March

As the icy winds of March howl about your tiny ears, and you urge the huskies on with cries of, "On, Nanook! 'Tis but another mile to Tesco's and we need more fish fingers," what thoughts lurk at the back of your frozen brain?
- **a.** *!!??*!! XXX!!*!! winter!!!!
- **b.** Hot buttered crumpets and JAM!!!
- **c.** Soon it will be SPRING, and I'll make eighteen new summer dresses and pick daffodils and teach the huskies to water-ski.

April

Your little brother rouses you from your morning zuzz by galloping into your room waving his best atomic ray-gun and shrieking, "The Martians have landed!!!" What do you do???
- **b.** Grunt, "April Fool," and go back to sleep.
- **c.** Go out and organise a treaty which gives you gold-mining rights on Saturn, Neptune and the third moon of Pluto in exchange for one flying saucer load of dandelions per year. Then make breakfast.
- **a.** Wonder why they bothered.

May

The leaves are growing green upon the trees, the blossoms are blossoming and the birds are singing . . . And you are . . .
- **c.** opening your third boutique specialising in swimwear, suntan oil, cold drinks and cures for sunstroke?
- **a.** mumbling, "Yes, well, it's all right now, but it'll be snowing when *I* go on holiday, it always does"?
- **b.** trying to remember where you put your sunhat last October?

June

June is sizzling away out there, but you've got to work. How do you deal with this difficult situation?
- **a.** ZZZZZZZZ.
- **c.** By getting up at six, so I can have a swim and a game of tennis before breakfast, and then I can sunbathe at lunchtime and go out on the river in the evening, and . . .
- **b.** By shifting my desk into the sunny bit by the window and working like mad when the sun goes in . . .

£1·50

contents

Printed and Published in Great Britain by D. C. Thomson & Co., Ltd., 185 Fleet Street, London EC4A 2HS   © D. C. Thomson & Co., Ltd., 1980.
ISBN 0 85116 183 9

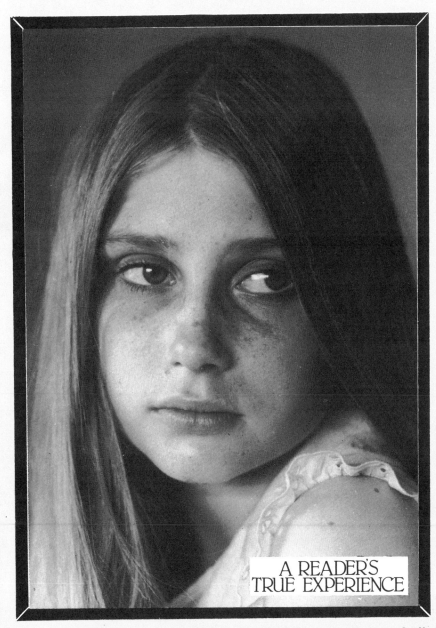

The sky was black and the waves were pounding, and all I could think of was Danny and the quarrel we'd had the night before. But the sea had already taken my father – surely it couldn't claim another sacrifice from me . . .

We Didn't Even Say Goodbye...

THE wind was already starting to blow when I came in from doing Mum's shopping in the village, and great black clouds were rolling in, threatening rain. Away across the salt marshes, white tops were beginning to appear on the waves and for a moment I stood at the gate watching them. Then, as the memories suddenly surged up in my mind, I turned away and went back inside.

"Looks as though there's a real storm brewing," Mum said as I put the shopping bag down on the kitchen table. "I hope all the boats get back in before it gets too bad!"

I forced a smile. "Oh, they will, don't worry," I said with a lightness I didn't feel. "Most of them have got radios now. They'll get plenty of warning!"

"Yes, but . . ." Mum's voice tailed off, but though the words were unsaid, I saw the sadness in her eyes and I knew what was going through her mind — memories of Dad and what had happened to him and his boat in a storm this time last year. I knew she was thinking that sometimes even the most modern scientific equipment isn't enough if the sea is determined . . .

Wanting to keep those thoughts out of my own mind too, I changed the subject quickly, and started to talk about a dress I'd seen in town the day before. I said I thought I'd buy it for a party I was going to with Danny the following week.

"If you've made your quarrel up by that time!" Mum said sharply. "I thought you told me yesterday that it was all over between you."

"That was yesterday!" I told her. "We'll make it up when he comes round tonight, you see if we don't!"

"If he gets home in time!"

"If he gets home at all!"

Fear

Gran's voice startled me — I hadn't heard her come into the kitchen — and my voice shook a little as I asked her what she meant.

She smiled coldly. "You know very well what I mean, Sue," she said then. "It's what I've always said — you should never let your man go to sea when there's anger in your heart. You should never let him go without saying goodbye . . ."

She looked straight at Mum as she finished speaking and I knew what Gran was thinking — Mum and Dad had had a quarrel, too, on the night before he was drowned and he had gone out without saying goodbye . . .

These memories added to my fear and I felt I couldn't bear to stay in the house a moment longer.

Grabbing my coat, I set out, but already the wind was stronger, and I could hardly keep my balance.

"Danny, please come back safely!" I whispered, but the wind carried my words away.

Memories of all the good times I'd had with Danny came flooding into my mind. All the times we'd walked down here together, hand in hand, happy and laughing. I tried to tell

continued overleaf 5

continued from
previous page

myself it'd be like that again, that he'd come home safe from the storm. But memories of my dad were strong in my mind. I remembered how Mum and I had sat and waited through that other storm, how we'd each tried to tell the other that Dad would get back safely. And how we'd both been wrong.

I knew I couldn't bear to lose Danny the same way and I forced myself to go on, down to the shore, to look out to sea for some sign of the boat, as though by seeing him I could make him safe.

But there was nothing out there.

"Danny!" His name came out like a sob as Gran's words went echoing round in my mind again and I thought of how I'd let him go last night when there was anger in my heart. He'd been angry, too, so that neither of us had said goodbye. I'd just taken it for granted then that he'd come back to me tonight, that we'd kiss and make up, the way we'd done with all our quarrels in the past. But now, it seemed I wasn't going to get the chance . . .

Desolate

Tears began to trickle down my cheeks as I turned back towards the cottage. I felt desolate. And then the rain began to pour down, soaking me through before I could get home.

"Any news?" I asked Mum as I got in, but she shook her head.

"Not yet," she said. "But it's still early — they might have gone in to another harbour or they might be sitting it out on the open sea. It depends where they were when the storm blew up."

"I suppose so." I knew she was trying to comfort me, but somehow I couldn't believe her.

The evening dragged on and I just couldn't settle to watch TV with Mum and Gran. I went up to my bedroom and shut the door, needing to be alone . . .

I kept trying to imagine what the future would be like without Danny, but I couldn't do it. He'd been part of my life for so long.

When someone started hammering at the front door, my heart seemed to stop beating. I knew it was for me, but I couldn't bear to go down and find out. I didn't want to hear the news. I just couldn't take it. I knew I couldn't.

When Mum called for me to go down, my legs felt so weak I could hardly stand up. There was a cold, sick feeling in my stomach and my hands were shaking uncontrollably.

"Who is it?" I asked as I got into the hall. "What's happened . . .?"

Then suddenly he stepped out of the shadows and I saw him.

"Danny!" And suddenly the tears that were streaming down my face were tears of joy. "Danny, I was so worried. I thought — I thought . . ."

But he wouldn't let me tell him what I thought. He was too busy pulling me into his arms and kissing me. And, as I clung to him, I knew that in future, I'd never let him go again without saying goodbye . . .

6

JUST GOOD FRIENDS?

Having a "boy friend" doesn't have to spell romance – or does it ?

SOME of my best friends are blokes. In fact, to be honest, out of all the people I know, I've only got one close female friend – while there must be at least half a dozen fellas I've rushed to in my hour of need!

But I once lost a boy "friend" for good when he turned into a "boy-friend" and we had a quick romance together.

While it lasted, it was great – but when it was over, so was the "friendship." We just couldn't get back to the easy-going friendship we'd had before the kisses and cuddles had interrupted us, simply because they **had** interrupted us, and whenever we looked at each other we remembered that and felt kind of embarrassed and sad.

So, how about boys as Best Friends? The advantages are enormous!

If you know a fella who you get on really well with as a friend, who you

something, so you could find yourself comforting **her**. This might take your mind off your own problems for a bit, but'll end up leaving you feeling a bit resentful 'cos she didn't listen to **you**.

IF you go to a boy friend, on the other hand, you're likely to get a much more level-headed reaction!

Maybe he won't pat your hand, but, because fellas are a lot more logical, he'll probably ask you sensible questions about why Jimmy has walked off into the great blue yonder. Then you'll have to try to give him answers – and in doing that you'll start thinking less fuzzily. You may, for example, hear yourself explaining that you've been rowing, that Jimmy said he was sick of the way you could never be on time, and **you** said you were sick of the way he kept nagging . . .

"A boy friend will give you a glimpse of how other boys behave and react . . ."

can talk to seriously when you have to, joke around with when you're in the mood, and just generally treat as if he were your own brother, then you're on to a winner, especially when it comes to things like your own romance busting up!

Well, picture it. You've been going out with Jimmy for weeks. Then suddenly he gives you the old heave-ho. Your first reaction is to burst into tears and vow you'll hate all men for ever more. Your second reaction is likely to be to go and find a shoulder to cry on.

If you go to a girl friend, she may well listen sympathetically, pat you on the hand and give you sound advice. She may even suggest you stay with her for a couple of days, till you feel a bit better, so she's a friend worth having. **But** she may also be having problems with her own fella, or have just rowed with her mum or

Once you've actually said all that, you're halfway to realising just why you actually split up – which means you're starting to look at things less emotionally. It **also** means you're starting to get over Jimmy!

Girl friends can, and do, help in similar situations. But somehow they tend to think the same way you do.

Boy friends, on the other hand, **because** they're boys, can often explain more clearly, and give you a glimpse of how **other** boys behave and react – which is always useful!

But a boy friend is less likely to put up with you being all moody for weeks on end than a girl friend is! Girl friends know all the different emotions that're going through you, and will be a lot more sympathetic – simply 'cos they can remember how they felt when it happened to them!

Boy friends, though, are a lot more useful when somebody you don't

fancy in the slightest is chasing you! A boy who's a friend can spell out that you just don't want this guy around a lot more successfully than a girl could! (A boy, who's a friend, can also threaten to **thump** the offending party, while a girl might have to be content with just kicking him on the ankle!)

Boys are also great at acting as a go-between if there's somebody you **do** fancy but are too shy to go after! A friend, particularly if he's also a friend of the guy you're drooling about, can say the right words in the right ear much more easily than a girl could. Girls tend to giggle when it comes down to this kind of thing – and then nobody takes them seriously!

HOWEVER, having a best friend who's a girl can often be a much easier relationship than having a best friend who's a boy. You and another girl know where you stand, right from the first moment you decide you're friends. You and a boy have to make sure you're both on the same wavelength, so neither of you ever gets the idea things are turning more serious, or more romantic, than they really are.

Remember, a boy who's a best friend has feelings, too. There'll be times when he'll want to talk to **you** about **his** problems – and he'll expect you to take him just as seriously as he's taken you in the past. So you've got to respect his confidences just the same way you would a girl friend's.

If you start going out with a new fella, make sure he understands about your "boy friend," otherwise he could wind up getting all jealous 'n' hot under the collar, and then start imagining you're two-timing him!

Obviously, you wouldn't have this problem if your best friend was a girl. But if it's a bloke, explain that your friend is just a friend. Introduce them to each other, let them get to know each other – if you don't, you could create a lot of problems for yourself!

THERE is, though, a definite **danger** to having boys as best friends. If you've known him for ages, if you're really close to him – but not on a romantic level – you're going to feel at ease with him whatever the circumstances. So it's all too easy, when you start out on a new romance, to compare the new guy to your best friend. You can find yourself wondering why your new fella doesn't act and react the way your friend does – and it's only one short step from that to actually beginning to wonder if you're **really** in love with your mate! But try to bear in mind that you can't **possibly** compare someone you've known for ages to someone you've only known 24 hours! Your new guy needs a chance!

And what if you **do** fall for your best friend? If the pair of you meet up for a moan one night – and end up in each other's arms?

Well, if it **does** happen, keep reminding yourself that there's very little about you he doesn't already know! You've told him practically all your secrets in the past – and vice versa!

You **could** have a happy-ever-after affair, but when two people know each other as well as you two do, it's terribly easy – in an argument or a row – for someone to come out with remarks about the past that can be really cruel or hurtful.

Best friends always know each other's weakest spots, and you'll be a lot more hurt if the guy you've finally decided you love suddenly turns round and yells, "Yeah, but I remember how **Jimmy** was always sick of you being late, too!" than you would be if a fella you'd only been going out with for a couple of weeks shouted, "Why can't you ever be on time?"

"It can ruin everything if a boy friend turns into a boyfriend . . ."

FRIENDSHIPS are tricky things. But a really good, close friendship is just about the most important thing in the world. If there's someone you know you can always turn to, someone you trust completely, then that person is worth his (or her) weight in gold.

So think twice before you turn a friendship into a romance. If it works, it'll be the greatest thing ever.

But if it **doesn't** work – you could lose something very, very special.

When Mum and I argued it was always about the same thing . . .

JO! WHERE ON EARTH HAVE YOU BEEN? YOU WERE SUPPOSED TO BE MEETING CAROL AND JANE AT THE ICE RINK TONIGHT. I'M GETTING FED-UP MAKING EXCUSES FOR YOU. I DON'T KNOW WHY YOU CAN'T BE MORE LIKE PAT—SHE NEVER LET ANYONE DOWN IN HER LIFE.

GIVE'S A BREAK, MUM. THE LAST THING I WANT IS TO END UP LIKE MY SISTER! IMAGINE GETTING MARRIED AT EIGHTEEN TO YOUR CHILDHOOD SWEETHEART, AND HAVING YOUR FIRST BABY BEFORE YOU'RE TWENTY. ALAN AND PAT NEVER GET OUT TO ENJOY THEMSELVES.

I've Been So Stupid...

ANYWAY, I HAD TO MISS THE SKATING SESSION! STEVE SUDDENLY ASKED ME TO GO TO THE DISCO. I COULDN'T SAY NO— HE MIGHT'VE THOUGHT I'D STOPPED FANCYING HIM.

YOU'RE IMPOSSIBLE! BUT ONE OF THESE DAYS YOU'LL LAND YOURSELF IN DEEP TROUBLE. JUST YOU WAIT AND SEE.

I never took any notice of Mum. I was too wrapped up in Steve.

SO, THERE I WAS, DIVING INTO THE POOL WHEN I REMEMBERED I'D LEFT A BUNSEN BURNER ON IN THE CHEMISTRY LAB!

WHAT DID YOU DO, YOU LUNATIC?

I HAD TO RUN ALL THE WAY BACK STILL WEARING MY SWIMSUIT.

YOU MUST'VE LOOKED LIKE A REAL WET!

And when he left her that night . . .

STEVE LIKES THE WAY I AM. HE'D HAVE FINISHED WITH ME LONG AGO IF I ACTED ALL SENSIBLE LIKE PAT.

And then, one Saturday afternoon . . .

I WONDER WHY THAT PRAM'S SITTING OUTSIDE OUR FRONT DOOR?

I'M GLAD YOU REMEMBERED TO GET BACK EARLY, JO. PAT AND I ARE ONLY GOING INTO TOWN TO LOOK AT SOME CURTAIN MATERIAL. BUT WE WON'T BE LONG.

WH- WHAT DO YOU MEAN?

DON'T TELL ME YOU'VE FORGOTTEN THAT YOU PROMISED TO BABY- SIT THIS AFTERNOON.

OH, NO! I SAID TO STEVE I'D GO WITH HIM TO THE FOOTBALL.

WELL, GET HIM TO COME ROUND HERE AND LISTEN TO RECORDS INSTEAD. I CAN'T GET THE PRAM ON THE BUS AND I'M NOT MISSING OUT ON MY MATERIAL SO, THIS TIME, YOU'LL HAVE TO KEEP YOUR PROMISE.

I thought Steve would be furious but he was really nice about it . . .

WHO WANTS TO STAND ABOUT IN THE COLD AND WATCH FOOTBALL ANYWAY? I'D MUCH RATHER BE WITH YOU.

COME OVER HERE AND SIT BESIDE ME.

SO YOU CAN KISS ME AGAIN? OK, IT'S A DEAL.

OH, STEVE, I LOVE YOU SO MUCH. I'D DO ANYTHING TO PLEASE YOU. YOU'RE SUCH GOOD FUN, BUT WHEN WE'RE ON OUR OWN YOU CAN BE SO ROMANTIC, TOO . . .

Continued on page 12

9

GET READY FOR FUN IN '81!

Is 1981 going to be *your* year? Find out in our star-studded special horoscope feature!

ARIES

It's a good year if you're going steady. Your boyfriend will prove he's responsible, reliable — the faithful type, in fact. He may seem a mite dull with it, but he *is* worth holding on to!

Sparks will fly in more casual romantic relationships. You're one of the zodiac's firebrands, and in 1981 you seem to attract boys even bossier than you.

Good news comes from abroad and you'll be spending time with foreign friends.

TAURUS

1981 starts well, with Cupid at your command, and you could cast a few spells here, there and everywhere.

As the year goes on, your love of freedom could cause a split between you and a steady boyfriend. You don't really want to cut loose completely, but you may be worried about that rut you're getting into.

You could spend quite a bit of time this year on a creative hobby — possibly dressmaking or design.

CANCER

Cupid scores a direct hit on your heart several times this year — and often when romance is the last thing on your mind!

You'll tend to see guys through rose-coloured glasses and be disappointed when you discover that any resemblance to Sting is only on the surface.

It's likely you'll make new boyfriends through working on some project, or a shared interest in animals.

GEMINI

Romance-wise, the year begins with soft lights, sweet music, and magic moments. You'll be confident, but cautious with it — no way is anybody going to sweep you off your feet!

Sports are well starred, too. You could be writing about them, if not taking part, reporting athletic events for a school or college mag maybe. Altogether 1981 is going to be a big improvement on 1980. Aren't you the lucky one!!

LEO

There'll be lots of ups and downs romance-wise. Some guys will try to fool you with flattery, but make sure you take all that sweet talk with a pinch of salt.

Often you'll feel you're soaring up to Cloud Nine, only to come down to earth with a painful bump.

Neighbours could help you get lucky, and the boy next door may improve on closer acquaintance! The local scene is changing, and although some mates are moving on, others are moving in.

VIRGO

In 1981 you'll be even more cautious and on your guard against becoming too involved when the year begins. But someone's generosity makes you take a shine to him, especially as you'll probably both be busy with some special project.

Original ways of making some spare cash will have a strong appeal for you, and the stars hint that you could be into photography, local history or antiques.

LIBRA

Steady relationships are well starred, and if you're going around with one particular boy just now, this romance will become warmer and stronger.

If there's more than one person you're keen on, though, you've really got problems, as this will cause a lot of jealousy since both boys want to be your one-and-only. So it's make-your-mind-up time!

You'll form some warm and sincere friendships. Probably you and your mates will be switched on to yoga, meditation, or a similar interest which helps you unwind.

SAGITTARIUS

Venus in Sagittarius gives 1981 a romantic start and there's no lack of magic moments these starry nights!

As the year goes on you may imagine yourself in love more than once, but you'll be seeing guys through rose-coloured glasses instead of as they really are.

You rely a lot on your more practical friends as you tend to drift and dream through the days. They'll be particularly helpful in class when you've no idea what teacher said 'cos you're so wrapped up in that hazy, lazy daydream world of your own.

CAPRICORN

Your popularity takes an upward swing in early spring, and before January is out romance puts stars in your eyes.

General trends in 1981 are anything and everything but dull, with lots of boys entering your life — and leaving it too! Some of them will be moving on but before you've waved one guy goodbye you'll be switched on to another.

SCORPIO

You'll attract plenty of attention, that's for sure! It's the year of the yo-yo when you hit the heights and plumb the depths as you fall in and out of love. Some of your dates in 1981 will be rather unusual, and you'll enjoy every minute of it all! You'll have to watch that reckless streak of yours, though, and be careful of the company you keep if you want to end 1981 with no regrets.

PISCES

You won't be content to drift with the tide this year, letting your mates decide on the action and following their lead.

Instead, you'll take time out to follow your own interests in art, music, poetry, and maybe keeping tropical fish. You'll meet some dishy fellas at the aquarists' club too.

You have shy moods, it's true, but if boys take you for a sweet-shrinking violet, this just shows what a good actress you are! Really, you can be very strong-willed and you could give one certain guy a shock.

AQUARIUS

This year is better than last, date-wise, but the road to romance is still bumpy. A few guys are going to throw stardust in your eyes and try to blind you to their faults with flattery.

It's important to make your head rule your tender heart, so if anyone keeps breaking dates — cut loose and forget him.

You'll meet some fascinating fellas through joining clubs catering for your many interests, which could range from bird-watching to scanning the skies in the hope of spotting UFOs.

Continued from page 9

We must have lost all track of time . . .

HEY, WHAT HAPPENED TO THE MUSIC?

I SWITCHED IT OFF. I WANT TO KNOW WHERE YOU'VE PUT THE BABY. IT WAS GOOD OF YOU TO BRING HIM INSIDE WHEN IT STARTED TO RAIN, BUT—

HAS IT BEEN RAINING? WE NEVER NOTICED.

WHAT D'YOU MEAN, YOU NEVER NOTICED? WHERE'S MARTIN? WHERE IS HE . . .

OH, PAT, I-I . . .

Suddenly, Jo's Mum appeared . . :

HE'S NOT IN EITHER OF THE BEDROOMS, OR IN THE KITCHEN, OR . . .

OH, NO, YOU DON'T THINK SOMEONE'S TAKEN HIM, DO YOU? WE'D BETTER CALL THE POLICE!

YOU SELFISH, IRRESPONSIBLE FOOL! WHAT HAVE YOU DONE?

CALM DOWN, PAT. STEVE'S GOT THE RIGHT IDEA. MAYBE THE POLICE WILL HAVE SOME INFORMATION.

But the police knew nothing . . .

HOW COULD I HAVE LEFT THE POOR LITTLE THING OUT HERE FOR SO LONG, WITHOUT CHECKING ON HIM?

IF—IF ANYTHING HAPPENS TO HIM, I'LL NEVER FORGIVE MYSELF.

Pat was out of her mind with worry.

WHAT AM I GOING TO TELL ALAN? HOW AM I GOING TO EXPLAIN THAT HIS LITTLE BOY ISN'T HERE ANY MORE?

DON'T GET SO UPSET, LOVE. THE POLICE ARE DOING ALL THEY CAN.

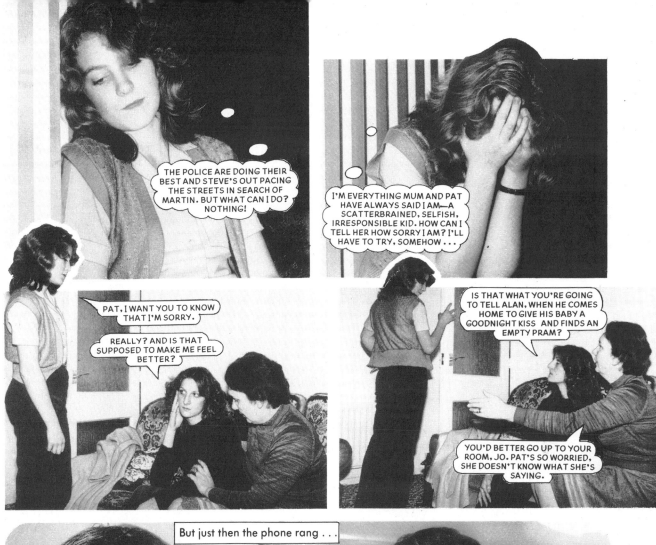

THE POLICE ARE DOING THEIR BEST AND STEVE'S OUT PACING THE STREETS IN SEARCH OF MARTIN. BUT WHAT CAN I DO? NOTHING!

I'M EVERYTHING MUM AND PAT HAVE ALWAYS SAID I AM—A SCATTERBRAINED, SELFISH, IRRESPONSIBLE KID. HOW CAN I TELL HER HOW SORRY I AM? I'LL HAVE TO TRY, SOMEHOW...

PAT, I WANT YOU TO KNOW THAT I'M SORRY.

REALLY? AND IS THAT SUPPOSED TO MAKE ME FEEL BETTER?

IS THAT WHAT YOU'RE GOING TO TELL ALAN, WHEN HE COMES HOME TO GIVE HIS BABY A GOODNIGHT KISS AND FINDS AN EMPTY PRAM?

YOU'D BETTER GO UP TO YOUR ROOM, JO. PAT'S SO WORRIED, SHE DOESN'T KNOW WHAT SHE'S SAYING.

But just then the phone rang...

THIS IS SERGEANT FRASER. WE'VE GOT YOUR GRANDSON. A YOUNG WOMAN HAS JUST BROUGHT HIM IN— SHE'D BEEN GRIEVING FOR HER OWN DEAD CHILD AND WHEN SHE SAW MARTIN SHE COULDN'T RESIST HIM.

THANK GOODNESS HE'S ALL RIGHT.

DRY YOUR TEARS NOW, PAT. I WANT TO SEE YOU PUT ON A BIG SMILE FOR MARTIN, WHEN WE GET TO THE POLICE STATION. ALL'S WELL THAT ENDS WELL, RIGHT?

FOR PAT, MAYBE.

BUT THERE'LL BE NO HAPPY ENDING FOR ME, UNLESS I CHANGE MY WAYS! IF I WANT TO MAKE ANYTHING OF MY LIFE, AND FIND THE KIND OF HAPPINESS PAT HAS FOUND WITH ALAN AND THE BABY I'LL NEED TO DO A LOT OF GROWING-UP.

THE END

THE GHASTLY TRUTH ABOUT TELLING THE TRUTH!

OK, this is the moment of truth. From now on, you've decided to fib no more, tell the truth, shame the devil, and astonish the life out of your family. You'll be admired, loved, feel a warm glow of virtue . . .

Well, let me tell you, folks, it won't work out like that!

You'll begin, of course, at home, in the midst of your own loving family.

When Mum asks, "Who on earth managed to get marmalade all over the gerbil? And who filled little Cyril's wellies with cornflakes?" you won't say (as you used to) "Gosh, dunno, but the cat's been acting awfully funny this week. Remember how it pulled the knob off the telly last Thursday?"

No! Wide-eyed with innocence, you'll cry, "Cyril and Angela decided to give the gerbil breakfast in bed. But the ungrateful beast didn't like the cornflakes and what's more he fell asleep on the toast and marmalade."

Then you can sit back, feeling virtuous and good, waiting for your just reward. This should arrive in about three minutes when Cyril kicks you on the shins, Angela sets fire to your new *Blue Jeans* and your mum tells you to stop making trouble and clean out the gerbil's cage. Finally, to add injury to insult, the ungrateful animal'll savage your thumb.

They don't *understand*, of course, families never do. But fear not, (poor, reckless fool that you are), out in the big wide world people'll appreciate your honest face. Like at school, for instance.

When they see how radiantly truthful you have become, you'll be moved to the top of the class, be let off sums, and there'll be a half-holiday in your honour every Thursday, won't there? Oh, no, there won't!

This is what'll really happen to you . . .

You'll trot in to school, smiling all over your face and everything'll be fine — until you open your tiny mouth. Then, before you know what's hit you you'll be in detention for 43 years. No-one'll speak to you. Mr Foskiss'll have turned purple and Miss Witherspoon'll be steaming at the ears.

"But I was only telling the *truth!*" you babble, as they lead you out in chains. And it's perfectly true, you were.

Cast your mind back to what you said . . .

"No, I haven't forgotten my homework, Mr Foskiss, I didn't actually do it because it was so

boring I fell asleep."

"*I've* seen your gym stuff, Agatha. Someone hid it under the bush just inside the main gates."

"Sir, you've forgotten to set us some homework."

"Miss Witherspoon, your wig's all gone funny at the back."

Well, it was all *true*. Um. Yes. Look, I don't think you've quite got the message yet. Maybe you'd better go off and see your friends (if you've still got any, that is!).

So you go off into town with three remaining friends.

Maud, your number-one friend, wants a new skirt. She tries on a slinky red pencil skirt, and she thinks it's *beautiful*. It isn't. It makes her look like a runaway pillar box.

So what do you say? Yes, that's right, *you* say, "It makes you look like a runaway pillar box." At this point Maud bursts into tears and says she'll never speak to you again.

This leaves you to go off for a coffee with *two* friends. One of them is truly in love with handsome Arthur, the fastest biker in the West. One day, she hopes,

he'll carry her off on his gleaming white motorbike. But you know he wouldn't look at her twice.

"Arthur said he'd never go out with you," you say, helpfully, "not with your spotty face."

This leaves you with a lapful of coffee, and *one* friend. But keep smiling, you haven't done anything wrong, it's just that people haven't yet learned to appreciate your brand new sincerity.

Your one remaining friend'll take you home to tea, and what happens? Well, the truth of it is, you'll leave at high speed three minutes later to the sound of shouting and smashing crockery.

Did you *have* to say, "But you weren't actually *at* the youth club on Wednesday, Doris. That's the night you went to that *terrible* place with Sneaky Sid. Don't you remember?"

Yes, I suppose you did have to tell the truth under the circumstances. But you should have known better.

Well, since you'll be leaving the district . . . (I did tell you you'd have to leave the district, didn't I? Well, you will, unless

you want to be lynched. The Third Bombchester Guide Troop are after you, and so are the Church Youth Club and the R.S.P.C.A.).

Yes, since you'll be leaving the district, I suppose you'd better look for a job. I think this could be a bit difficult, though, unless you change your ways a bit. I mean, at least wait until after the *interview* before you reveal your true shining self in all its glory.

Oh, well, you won't get the job. Not if you're going to tell them the absolute truth.

"I got the sack from the last place I worked 'cos they said I was the dumbest girl they'd met and if I'd stayed any longer, they'd go broke. But they did say I'm terribly honest."

So there you are, unemployed, broke and friendless. And that's after only a week of telling the truth.

At this point you'll finally discover the ghastly truth about telling the truth. Yes, that's right. There really are times when the truth is the very *last* thing that people want to hear!

"IT'S QUICKER BY TUBE!"

These smashing tubular chokers and bracelets would brighten up any outfit, and they're so quick and cheap to make, too!

For the **BLUE SAUSAGE** one you need: a strip of material 8 cm wide and 50 cm long. (We used Laura Ashley printed cotton.) Kapok for the stuffing and Velcro Touch 'n' Close fastener.

Fold the material in half lengthways with the right side inside and sew up the whole length. Turn the right way out and push the stuffing down inside the tube with a knitting needle till it's filled apart from 2½ cm at either end. Sew across the tube at the end of the stuffing, then fold ½ cm to the inside at the outer edges and sew them up.

You've now got a flat, unstuffed section at either end. Stitch a piece of Velcro to each of these, one piece on the top side, the other on the underside. Press them together — and there's your choker.

For the matching bracelet make a tube about 25 cm long in the same way, but after you've stuffed it fold ½ cm to

the inside at one end. Then bend the other end round and stick it inside the opening. Sew the ends together like this.

If you fancy **GOLD AND SILVER SNAKES** circling your throat — here's how we made 'em. We used 55 cm of 2½ cm-wide gold braid and the same of silver. To make the tubes we simply folded the braid in half lengthways and oversewed the long edge. They were then stuffed with Kapok — but if you find this too fiddly you could try threading thick string down them instead.

The gold tube was sewn to

the silver one at one end, then they were twisted together before being sewn together at the other end. (Remember to leave 1 cm unstuffed at the tube ends so they can be easily sewn together by placing one of the flattened ends on top of the other.) Then Velcro was stitched on the ends.

The slinky bracelet was made from tubes 27 cm long. Gold and silver Sellotape was used to hold the ends together here. When the first, stuffed tube was bent into a circle we held it together with silver Sellotape. Then we twisted the second one round it before sticking it in place with gold Sellotape.

The **PLAITED RIBBON** choker in ice cream colours of pink, coffee and cream, started off as three 70 cm lengths of 2½ cm-wide satin ribbon. Each was made into a tube as for the blue sausage necklace, and the open ends were sewn up. All three tubes were laid side by side and sewn together 5 cm down from one end. Then they were plaited together, just as you plait hair, stopping 7 cm from the bottom.

The two outer tubes at the bottom end were tucked up 2½ cm to the inside of the plait and

sewn down in the middle. One half of a snap fastener was sewn on top of these ends, and the other half snap fastener sewn to the inside end of the middle tube. At the other end of the plait, the middle tube was turned 2½ cm to the inside and sewn down, and the two outside tubes were sewn together to form a loop. The necklace is fastened by slipping the long tube end through the loop and pressing the snap fasteners together. (If you'd rather use Velcro — just sew the tubes neatly together side by side at each end and sew the Velcro on top.)

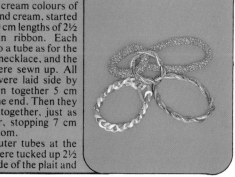

NAMES IN THE FRAMES

Who's top of your charts? Fix your eyes on the frame to see if you can pick out your fave pop people.

You'll find them in straight lines going backwards, forwards, up and down, or diagonally across the frame. We're giving you *Racey* to get you on the right track.

Check your score with the answers on page 60.

T	S	T	S	T	A	R	N	W	O	T	M	O	O	B
S	T	S	T	B	T	A	S	Q	U	E	E	Z	E	L
D	U	D	B	T	B	C	U	S	Q	U	E	Z	E	O
D	B	A	R	O	B	E	R	T	S	O	N	N	N	N
R	E	S	S	H	E	Y	E	C	T	N	E	N	A	D
A	W	E	E	N	O	P	E	C	I	L	O	P	N	I
H	A	L	E	X	N	O	X	E	O	H	P	N	I	E
C	Y	G	G	E	I	L	K	V	E	P	C	P	T	I
I	A	G	E	O	M	I	I	Y	R	U	D	N	A	I
R	R	U	E	N	U	C	M	I	Y	R	U	N	W	B
F	M	B	B	U	H	E	F	A	C	D	A	S	A	O
F	Y	G	L	O	R	I	A	G	A	Y	N	O	R	N
I	G	L	L	E	T	R	A	M	A	N	E	L	D	E
L	E	L	V	I	S	C	O	S	T	E	L	L	O	Y
C	N	O	S	K	C	A	J	L	E	A	H	C	I	M

WHO'S this steaming towards you across the floor, with pounding feet and rubber soles, eager to fling you over his shoulder or swing you round his head? No, it's not Bruce Lee or Spider Man, but the **Rocking Steam Roller**.

All drainpipes, blue suede shoes and greasy hair, this lad is highly energetic and can be rather dangerous if you're out of training. So if you're feeling a bit *delicate* tonight, make sure he doesn't get within grabbing distance of your ponytail, or your feet won't touch the ground again until 3 a.m.!

SO, how about *this* guy? Dressed neatly in the suit his mother got him from a five-year-old mail-order catalogue, he clumps across and begins to leap around in front of you. This rather wound-up lad is **Clockwork Clarence**, and he's frantically doing the steps he read in his mum's magazine — all three of them, hopelessly out of time.

In fact, the whole dance is a bit odd, the way it stops dead in the middle like that. This is because his mum gave the mag to the woman next door before he'd quite got the hang of the rest of the steps.

Anyway, he's impossible to dance with, so when your feet can take no more, gently point him in the opposite direction, and he'll frantically high-kick off, and never come near you again all evening . . . you see, he hasn't learned how to turn round yet!

WELL! What about this high-speed whizzer, copying steps from *Grease* with his left foot and *Saturday Night Fever* with his right, causing everyone to gaze at him in admiration? He's the one and only **Travolta Vaulter**, leaping about like crazy and trying to win an Olympic Gold Medal for advanced athletics. Wow, but this boy's a smasher — snappy white suit, snappy white teeth, film-star face and twinkling toes, all energy and grace . . . and as he flies about you, he makes you feel like a horse in diving boots!

This lad doesn't even *need* his partner — he's dancing for himself alone, though he does allow his fans to stand and watch him in silent admiration. Wander off, have a Coke and change your corn

The lights are low and the music plays, you're looking your best and raring to go — but wait a minute . . .

WHO'S YOUR DISCO KING?

lasters — he won't even notice you've gone . . .

BUT you'll notice the **Cow-hide Kid**. Well, it's pretty hard *not* to notice the clumsy oaf who's just knocked you off your chair!

He's dressed entirely in leather, covered in fringes, and has still got his crash-helmet on. He dances as if he's still on his motor-bike, only there're no indicators, so you don't know which way he's going next.

He's possibly quite nice, but it's hard to tell under all that biking gear — and he won't take it off 'cos it's so much bother putting it on again!

IF you haven't the energy to lug about all that leather, and you don't fancy learning the Cowhide Kid's own variety of Rollerball Disco, how about a whirl across the boards with **Flash Harry** here?

He's right up to the minute in his flash Sixties' suit (or is it a Fifties' suit?), his clipped hair and his corrugated cardboard shoes.

The difficulty about dancing with Harry is that he's doing a dance that no-one else has ever seen before! This is because he's just made it up. It's no good trying to learn it, because it's out of date as soon as he's done it.

No, it's useless trying to do the same dance as Harry, so why not make up *your* own dance as you go along? It may make him realise that you, too, are a genius. Then again, it might make him go off in a huff.

DEAR, oh dear, they're a pretty useless bunch really, when you look at them, leaping about there under the flashing lights. Not so much Disco Dynamite, more like Disco Discards. You don't know why you bothered to come, 'cos you might as well dance with that pillar in the corner, it'll pay you a bit more attention. Probably dance better, too . . .

But hang on, hang on, wait a minute . . . who's this dashing up out of the gloom and taking you by the lily-white hand? What's he look like? Blue jeans, clean pullover, and a great big smile? He's saying *hello*, and would you like to dance?

He isn't treading on your feet and he's doing the dance *you've* just learned to do??? He isn't throwing you about, and he isn't dancing on the opposite side of the room, and he hasn't suddenly vanished for a drink? You're sure? Well then, what are you waiting for? This is your very own **Blue Jeanius** — and when the music starts you'll *both* be Disco Dynamite!

So get cracking, twinkletoes!

yoga your way

YOGA has been around for over 5000 years, and for some people it's a whole way of life. But *you* can benefit by following just a few of the basic positions every day, as they are designed to exercise every muscle in the body. (You may even discover muscles you never knew you had!)

Take your time when doing the exercises and breathe in and out regularly and deeply. If you can't get into the positions at first don't try to force your body to do them, move on to the next exercise and after a few days' practice you'll find your body will have loosened up.

Try to find a quiet, airy room to exercise in and wear something comfortable. If you like, you can lie on a large towel for the floor exercises.

Flight —

This is a good exercise to begin with since it loosens you up, and as the blood rushes to your head you'll feel more alert and active.

a. Stand with your feet apart and your arms outstretched to the sides.

Breathe in and, thrusting your arms back, bend your body back as far as you can.

Hold this position for five seconds.

b. Breathing out, bend forward, keeping your arms outstretched behind you.

Hold for five seconds. Breathe in and bend backwards again. Repeat three times.

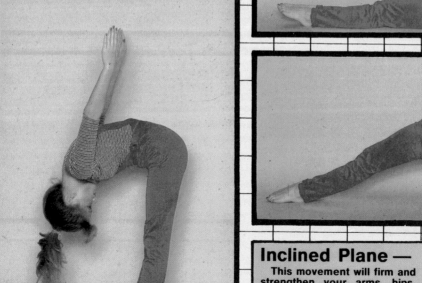

Inclined Plane —

This movement will firm and strengthen your arms, hips, back and thighs.

a. Sit with your legs outstretched, put your arms behind you, palms resting flat and fingers pointing away from your body.

b. Breathe in and raise up your body, resting your weight on your hands and feet.

Hold for five seconds, breathing freely. Lower your body back to the first position.

Repeat three times.

18

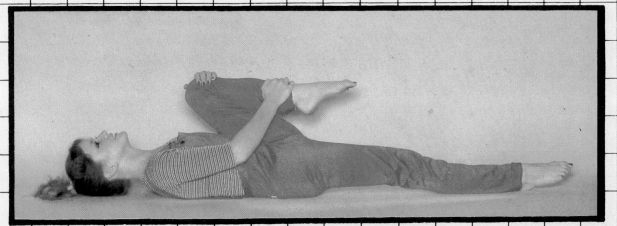

Dance Of The Legs —

Do this regularly and you'll soon have a firm tummy, bottom and thighs.

a. Lie flat on your back with your arms above you. Straighten your left leg and hold it up as high as possible. At the same time bring your arms up to grasp your left ankle.

b. Breathe out and, bending your leg, bring it close to your chest. Hold for five seconds. Breathe in and go back to the first position.

Repeat the exercise with your right leg.

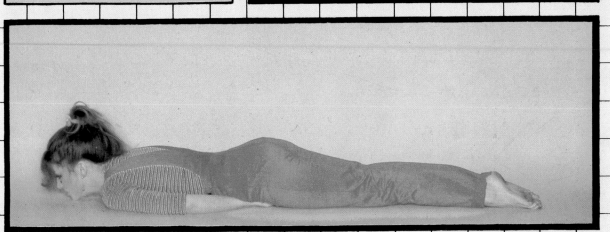

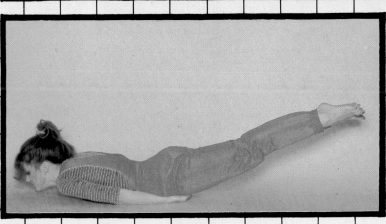

The Locust —

This trims and tones your tummy and also firms up your bottom, hips and thighs.

a. Lie face down on the floor with your legs together. Clench your fists and place them together, underneath you.

b. Breathe in deeply and, pressing your fists against the floor, thrust your legs up as high as possible, keeping your head down and your knees straight. Hold this position for five seconds. Breathe out and lower legs.

Repeat three times.

Hip Stretch —

This one's great for trimming and firming your waist and the inside of your thighs.

Stand up straight with your feet far apart and your hands on your thighs.

Turning your right foot out, bend your right knee and rest your right hand on it.

Stretch your left leg away from you until your left knee is perfectly straight, and place your left hand on the side of your left thigh. Breathe in and hold this position for five seconds. Breathe out and return to standing position keeping your legs apart. Repeat the exercise bending your left knee.

Repeat three times.

Four-Way Stretch —

This tones up your waist, legs and arms and expands your lungs.

a. Stand straight with your feet together and your arms at your sides.

Breathe in deeply and raise your hands above your head, interlocking your fingers. Holding your breath, stretch upward on tiptoe.

b. Breathe out and bend forward, touching the floor if you can.

c. Breathe in and come back to standing position with your arms raised.

Hold your breath. Bend to the left and to the right without bending your elbows. Hold positions each time. Stretch upward on tiptoe. Lower your arms, breathe out and relax.

Repeat twice.

Shoulder Stand Variations —

This is to make your spine supple and improve your circulation.

a. Go up on your shoulders with your legs straight up in the air. Support your back with your hands. Breathe in and bend your right knee. Hold, straighten your leg, breathe out, and do the same with your left leg.

b. Breathe in and lower both legs over your head without bending your knees until your toes touch the floor behind you. Hold. Breathe out and return to vertical position. Slowly lower your legs until you're lying on the floor.

The Stoop —

This'll improve your posture as well as trimming up your tummy and thighs.

a. Kneel down, tucking your legs under your bottom and with your spine straight. Interlock your fingers behind your back. Breathe in deeply and stretch your arms backwards and outwards.

b. Breathe out as you bend forward until your head touches the floor. Keep your arms straight up behind you and make sure your hips don't come off the ground. Breathe freely and hold the position for five seconds. Breathe out and slowly come back to the kneeling position.

Repeat twice.

SECTION ONE

Right from the very beginning there are signs designed to help you. Even in the identification of your new fella. It could be he's got . . .

a one-track mind,

a several-track mind but all going in the same direction,

or no mind at all!

He could be a bit of a dear,

or a bit of a drip.

If he looks great in tight jeans

and sees you home after every date,

thinks you're prettier than Raquel Welch

and Anna,

then hang on to this guy,

'cos fellas that well trained

don't fall into your lap every day!

SECTION TWO

Fellas have developed a very noticeable warning system involving changing colours.

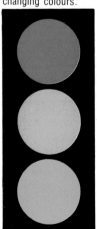

RED: They may be a little embarrassed. Stop calling him coochy-cuddles in front of all his mates.

AMBER: Ah. A happy medium. It shows your relationship is bang on course, balanced right down the middle. Then again, maybe he's got jaundice!

GREEN: Whoops! Jealousy! Stop makin' eyes at every good-looking Alfie Romeo you pass.

Flashing green men should be avoided at all times as they usually come from Mars and are disgustingly rude!

The Guy-Way Code

Follow our fellow-bricked-road to success!

OK, so you've got yourself a boyfriend. A life-time escort. And you're looking forward to rolling along life's highway together.

But are you quite ready for its twists and turns? D'you know in which direction you're headed, and can you recognise the hazards and danger signs ahead on the rocky road to love?

If you're in any doubt at all, then this special BJ feature is just for you . . .

HANDY HINT – 1

To help with your driving (driving your fella crazy, that is) use your mirror as much as possible to ensure that you always look your best!

SECTION THREE

If you're guy is a bit of a saucy character

and there is a kissing manoeuvre approaching,

remember, no matter what he says, you needn't

to all of his suggestions. You can immediately pull him up with a loud

or a hefty left hook!

HANDY HINT – 2

Too many crisps and sweets between meals affects your weight.

22

SECTION FOUR

Beware of overtaking your fella completely as this might scare him off.

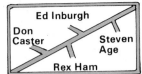

Let him spend some time with his mates

and have some hobbies of his own, like

stunt-riding,   football,   rugby   or weight-lifting.

HANDY HINT – 3

Kissing for long periods can make you drowsy. To avoid this, stop every twenty minutes to get some fresh air.

SECTION FIVE

Most fellas have had previous owners (called mothers). To win mums over to your side do not say, "Where did you get that awful hat?"

Or, "I hear you can be a bit of a nag . . ."

It's advisable to give little pressies, like liquorice allsorts

and fruit pastilles.

Also, praise how well she makes cups of

and apologise for knocking yours over as you sat down!

SECTION SIX

If your fella turns out, sadly, to be the over-possessive type,

PRIVATE PROPERTY
HANDS OFF

has bad dandruff

and goes wild if you even talk to another guy,

give him the big elbow immediately

and find someone who moves on your wavelength.

HANDY HINT – 4

Remember the old Chinese proverb: "Boyfriend is like long motorway in fog. The less turn-offs the better!"

SECTION SEVEN

You *must* learn the warning signs that indicate your fella might be interested in another girl.

Meter ZONE

Don't let him hang out at Meter Zones. If he's looking for a new owner, this is where he'll meet 'er.

If his eyes have started to wander

and his mind is

ELSEWHERE

you could be in for fireworks and trouble.

So tell him to get on his

and get lost!

And there we are. Simple isn't it? Just master these signs and warnings, and your love life should be plain sailing all the way to the

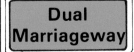

Dual Marriageway

He can drive you round in a flashy car to all the smart places. He can give you anything money can buy.

I can give you love, Kelly, and caring and warmth and gentleness.

But neither of us can give you time...

TOO LATE FOR OUR LOVE...

I KNOW you're laughing at me, Kelly, as you sit over there with your new friends, glancing across at me every so often with that sneer on your face.

What happened to us, Kelly? What happened to our love?

We grew up here, in this little village, before "the townies" discovered how beautiful it was. We both called them "townies." Everybody else in the village did, too, at first. We all thought that the village was being spoilt.

Remember how Mr Jones, from the General Stores, used to rage at the strange things they asked for in his shop, the way they always pushed their way to the front of the crowd of friendly, chatting villagers, demanding to be served.

"That holiday cottage site ought to be burned to the ground. Luxury houses indeed!" he'd snarl into his moustache. "I wish their manners were luxury, too . . ."

It's strange, now, to see his newly-painted supermarket, shining as brightly as the summer sun, its windows advertising all the latest bargains. I've not heard him complain for years, except in the winter, when his sales go down.

"Nice people," he says, "those from the cottages!"

We weren't going to change

They've all turned out like that, all the older folk. They've got used to the changes, to the disco in the old village pub, to the cabin cruisers and smart little sailing boats crowding our peaceful bay and spoiling the fishing. They like the money it brings in. They like feeling as if they're all a part of the new scene.

"Got to change with the times," you hear them say.

But we weren't going to change, were we, Kelly? Didn't we make plans about staying around, staying together, making sure that everything was always the same? That late summer, when we realised that our childhood friendship had turned to love, we sat on the gorse-covered hill, staring out over a still blue sea, planning our life here, deciding that new ways and new people had nothing to do with us.

I remember you that day, Kelly. You weren't sneering then. You were sitting, leaning forward, clutching your knees, your brown eyes burning, your quick bright smile lighting up your face. You told me you'd never leave here, that you'd help your dad on the farm, that this was all you wanted.

Then you turned to me, and I knew that *you* were all I wanted. I reached out to touch your cheek.

"And me, Kelly?" I murmured.

"I'll always be with you . . ." you whispered.

I took you in my arms then, and I told you I loved you. I meant it then, as I mean it now.

Why did you have to start despising me, and this life I'll never leave? I'm a fisherman, that's all. That's what my father was. I have no airs and graces. I'll not convert my boat to give pleasure trips to the tourists. I'll earn my living in a way I can be proud of.

I remember a time when you were proud of it, too.

All the long winter and spring we laughed and loved and talked about the future. Remember that day we dug one of your father's lambs out of the snow-drift, that day we wondered whether summer would ever come?

You looked so tired, waiting for the sun, tired and pale and thin. I thought the winter had been too long for you, that summer would bring back my sunshine girl.

But summer brought the tourists. And Paul Ferris.

We'd seen him before, of course. He'd been coming to the village for a few years. He was one of the crowd we had nothing to do with. He was everything we said we hated, brash, trendy, loud when he talked, louder when he laughed. How could you have fallen in love with him, Kelly?

You didn't tell me

Perhaps it was the clothes and the money. He dressed well, drove a little sports car, and bought drinks for everyone in sight. He bought us a drink that night we wandered into the Mariner's Arms because you wanted a change.

I'd been worried about your restlessness since the beginning of the summer. Those things we'd loved to share had begun to mean less and less to you.

You'd started to complain about the hours I had to work, and the rough work you had to do most of the time. You told me about the part-time job you'd been offered, a waitress in the Yacht Club. You said that it would help to keep you occupied while I was out on fishing trips. I couldn't persuade you against it, nor could your dad.

I didn't like to see the way you were changing. Your eyes had a hard look in them and you began to yearn for all the things you'd never had, and had never wanted.

I knew when we went into the disco that night that it wasn't just a spur-of-the-moment decision. You'd tried so hard to look lovely that night, lovelier than usual, even though your faint summer tan was fading with the hours you spent inside, waiting on tables.

I thought you wanted to be beautiful for me. You knew I loved to see you in that yellow dress, like sunshine, like gorse, like the gleam of that golden ring I'd saved all my money for.

He looked at you as you came in on my arm, and I was proud for a moment that you were something he could never buy. Then you smiled at him, a close, secret smile, and I knew there was something between the two of you that there'd never been between us. The smile made my heart lurch with fear.

Worried

Then he walked over to you, to my girl, to the girl I wanted to spend my life with, and offered to buy us a drink. "For my favourite waitress and her little fisher boy!" he sneered. Your giggle sounded false and hollow.

It's the sound you're making now, as you sit on the terrace of the Yacht Club, chattering to your new friends, sitting so close to Paul Ferris. His arm lies around your shoulders. I know you're all looking at me down here, unloading my catch on to the quay.

Do you wonder what you ever saw in me, and in this village?

You didn't tell me for a month that it was all over between us. You let the summer stretch on, knowing that I couldn't lose hope, knowing that nothing you could do would make me stop loving you.

Continued Overleaf.

25

TOO LATE FOR OUR LOVE...

Continued From Previous Page.

You moved further and further away from me, closer and closer to the boy with the hard blue eyes and the white-blond hair. You started to tell me the funny things he said to you. He made you laugh, but he also taught you to sneer, Kelly.

Then you said you were leaving, that it was the end for you and me. You'd decided to move to the town, to find work in a shop or an office. You were tired of the farm, and tired of me. You said you wanted something more out of life than being shut away in a corner of nowhere. You said that you loved him.

You broke my heart.

I'll have to live without you

I can only watch you now, from a distance, as you move with the crowd. I see you swimming at the Yacht Club pool, thin and gaunt in your new bikini. It's fashionable to be slim, though, isn't it?

I see you clinging close to him as he drives that little green sports car through the narrow village streets.

I see you sitting with him in the Mariner's Arms. You're like a bright butterfly trapped in a shop window. You amuse them with your beauty and your eagerness and your local accent.

The ring I bought you lies dull in its box. I wonder if you'll ever wear it now.

You don't know, yet. I can tell that by the way you're planning a future that will never be.

I won't tell you. I can't. I want you to come back to me for love, because you can't go on without me.

I don't want you to come back to me in hopelessness and despair.

Your father told me, that day of the blizzard when we dug out the sheep and dragged it back to the safety of the fold. He asked me whether my feelings for you were real. I told him that I loved you and that I didn't think I could live without you.

He told me then, that I would have to. He told me to marry you at the end of the summer. He asked me to look after you and care for you because, he said, this summer would be the last you'd see.

He didn't want you to know that the illness that had killed your mother was in you, as well.

Night after night, Kelly, I cried, the way boys never do, knowing that the time we'd have together was so short. A lifetime of love would die in a year.

I'm watching you die, slowly, and I'm not with you to help and to love, and to let you share with me the beauty of this little place before it has nothing to give you any more.

You're going away from me, from all of us, from the gorse-covered hill and the peaceful blue of the sea. You're going to the smoke and the noise and the harsh bleakness of the town, to give what remains of your brightness to strangers.

I hope you'll realise before you go that I love you and that you're just a plaything to him. I hope you'll come running back to me, over the brow of the hill, before the autumn, to tell me that you've changed your mind.

I hope I can find the brightness in your eyes again. I hope I can give you hope at the end.

I want you to wear my ring, Kelly, before it's too late.

I have so much to give you, and so little time.

1. Tie yourself to a tree with it r time there's a hurricane.
2. Give it to your fella so you string him along . . .
3. Moor your boat to the batht with it, then it won't drift av when you pull the plug and the t goes out.
4. Learn to play the tin whistle, then do the Indian String tric
5. Astonish your friends! Cut it i four pieces, and put them in a hat with a white rabbit. S ABRACADABRA, and rem the rabbit. They will be *amazed* see that there are now four pie of string in the hat.
6. Tie yourself to somebody inter ing.
7. Twiddle it.
8. String your guitar with it, so y can practise at night without turbing the neighbours.
9. Crochet a useful wig with it.

10. Fasten it to an arrow, and fire t at the local chip shop. Usin second piece of string, lowe basket down it, containing message, "Haddock and ch please." (**N.B.** You need a l piece of string, and no corn between you and the chip sho
11. Darn your string vest with it. full of holes.
12. Use it to tie up a big parcel fu pressies for someone nice.
13. Tie your hat on with it.
14. Let it down from your bedro window with a note on, say "HELP!!!" Someone interest might come to your rescue.

BELIEVE IT OR KNOT

— we've come up with 33 wonderful things to do with a piece of string!

15. Cut it into three pieces, and plait it. Now you have a *plaited* piece of string.
16. Wrap it round and round and round and round the end of a piece of Blackpool rock, to make a nice non-sticky handle.
17. Use it as a handy substitute for spaghetti when someone you don't like comes to tea.
18. Use it to attach to your person all the various things you always leave behind, like your keys, gloves, sports kit, cheese sandwiches, etc.
19. Tie up your little brother with it.
20. Cut it in half. You now have *two* pieces of string for the price of one!!
21. Tie a bent pin to it, and catch dinner.
22. Keep it for a rainy day.

23. Play dog's cradle with it. (What? Well, *exactly* like cat's cradle, only different).
24. Use it to keep your jeans up when the zipper's gone.

25. Tie it to the mouse that climbs up the tower to the imprisoned prince, who then pulls up the string attached to the cord attached to the rope ladder, so he can climb down and carry you off on his white horse.
26. Put it in a box and give it to someone for Christmas.
27. Dye it green.
28. Lose it. Then when you find it again, you can tell it how much you missed it.
29. Mend a broken leg with it.
30. Swap it for something more interesting, like an old gobstopper.
31. Fry an egg with it. (Go on, use your imagination!)
32. Lasso an escaped rhinoceros with it.
33. Tie a knot in it to remind you to do all the things in this feature.

PICTURE THIS!

It's time for some of our top pop people to face the music as we tell you what their good looks really mean!

DAVID ESSEX

EYES: David's clear, sparkling eyes show that he's warm, lively and intelligent. He has lots of small laughter lines around his eyes which show his great sense of humour and he enjoys the company of people who can make him laugh.

EARS: Buried beneath all that hair, believe it or not, David has long, thick-lobed ears which show that he can also be cool and calculating, particularly where business is concerned, and when he doesn't like or approve of a thing, he'll say so in no uncertain terms!

NOSE: His small, broad nose reveals that he dislikes any kind of deception and cruelty, and can be over-generous, particularly if he thinks a person is in genuine need.

MOUTH: David's thin, well-shaped lips show that he's honest and outspoken, but he values his privacy almost too much sometimes.

CHIN: His strong chin reveals that he's adaptable and very willing to learn about everything and anything, and he's always interested and enthusiastic — particularly about new ideas.

JIMMY PURSEY

EYES: Jimmy's narrow eyes reveal that he's a bit suspicious of things and people he doesn't know, but he's also very intelligent and determined.

EARS: His slightly protruding ears show that he has a great sense of fun, but he's also a stay-at-home who's happiest in a domestic environment.

NOSE: Jimmy's strong nose reveals that he dislikes the "high life" and gets most pleasure and relaxation out of outdoor activities like fishing or playing football.

MOUTH: His rather large mouth reveals that he relies heavily on close friends, and they're among some of the most important things in his life. He'll always go to a few really close friends when he's in trouble, or tired, or simply depressed.

CHIN: His short, angular chin shows that he's a realist who likes to have his own way, and if he doesn't approve of a person or a situation he'll say so very directly. If he doesn't want to do a thing, he won't do it — and nothing and no-one will be able to make him.

BOB GELDOF

EYES: His large eyes show that he's intelligent and worldly-wise and he can sometimes be rather suspicious of people until he's 100 per cent sure of their motives.

EARS: His small ears show that he's slightly aggressive, and he finds it impossible to say or do flattering things if he doesn't believe in them.

NOSE: His wide and rounded nose shows that he has a great sense of fun and thoroughly enjoys relaxing by simply fooling around and playing practical jokes.

MOUTH: Bob's rather long, thin lips reveal that he can be very sarcastic and outspoken, but if he's asked for advice, he'll always be straightforward and reliable.

CHIN: His long, pointed chin shows that he finds it hard to unwind 'cos he has a restless, inquiring mind, and he's also a bit of a perfectionist:

DEBBIE HARRY

EYES: Debbie's heavy-lidded eyes show that she can be slightly suspicious and wary, particularly with people she doesn't know very well.

EARS: Her well-proportioned ears show that she's usually very easy-going, but she has enormous determination and drive, especially where her career is concerned. She's willing to try anything, and if at first she doesn't succeed — she just tries again!

NOSE: Her very straight nose shows Debbie's underlying aggressiveness which makes it hard for her to put up with people she doesn't like, and she hates being taken advantage of.

MOUTH: Debbie's mouth shows that she's sensual and sexy, and she has a woman-of-the-world appearance.

CHIN: Her very rounded chin shows that she relies on people she's close to, and because she's unsure of a great many things, she needs good friends she can turn to and depend on.

SHAKIN' STEVENS

EYES: His small, well-shaped eyes reveal that he knows himself very well and he's all too aware of his own limitations, both professionally and as a person.

EARS: His thick-lobed ears show that he's a warm person who cares about others a great deal, particularly those close to him. If a person is in trouble, he'll do all he can to help.

NOSE: Shakin's sharp, straight nose shows that he's essentially a home-lover who'll always be happiest with familiar things around him.

MOUTH: His narrow mouth shows that he's modest and shy and rather quiet. He can also be a bit sentimental and old-fashioned in his outlook sometimes.

CHIN: His neatly-shaped chin reveals that he enjoys success, but he's prepared to work hard for it, and is willing to do the same at anything he's interested in.

STING

EYES: His thin-lidded eyes show that he's intelligent and resourceful and he can be very sarcastic when he wants to be, but he's got a good and lively sense of humour, too.

EARS: His delicately-shaped ears reveal that he'd thoroughly enjoy a life of luxury. Being pampered and looked after appeals to him enormously, particularly when he has time to lie back and enjoy it.

NOSE: Sting's wide nose reveals that he's always alert, 'cos he dislikes wasting time and wants to get as much out of life as he can.

MOUTH: His narrow mouth shows that he can be impatient sometimes, but he's a good listener and a reliable friend.

CHIN: The strong bone-line of jaw and chin shows that he cares passionately about a lot of things, including his work, and he's extremely disciplined where that's concerned.

PAULINE BLACK

EYES: Pauline's large, very rounded eyes show that she can be slightly mistrustful and aggressive, and will always speak her mind, regardless of whether she hurts people or not.

EARS: Her delicate, well-proportioned ears reveal that she's neat, particularly about her own appearance, and has a slightly masculine attitude which is reflected in her own general, casual dress.

NOSE: Pauline's small snub nose shows that she's a fighter and she really dislikes being put into any one category, particularly by people whom she feels should know her better.

MOUTH: Her full, beautifully-shaped mouth shows that she has a sensitive, rather withdrawn side to her character which is always obvious, and she often feels insecure.

CHIN: Pauline's rounded chin shows that she's a very self-reliant person and thoroughly enjoys a good argument, but sometimes her temper can flare too quickly, and then she hurts even her closest friends.

PAUL WELLER

EYES: Paul's almond-shaped eyes show his forceful personality. When he feels strongly about something, he's never frightened to speak up.

EARS: His ears, which stick out a bit from his head, show that he dislikes anything that might be called "flashy" or false and he has passionate beliefs he'll always stick to.

NOSE: His long, straight nose shows that he's intelligent and far-seeing, and makes a loyal friend. He's also very warm-hearted and generous, but sometimes people take advantage of him.

MOUTH: His neatly-shaped, small mouth reveals that he's determined and aggressive, and can be very tough when he has to be. He tends to keep himself to himself a great deal, and he's a hard person to get to know well.

CHIN: His square-shaped chin shows that he hates insecurity of any kind, and although he has a good sense of humour, he also has a very quick temper which makes him do and say things he later regrets.

Yes, it's really amazing what these famous features can tell us — come to think about it, have you had a good look in the mirror lately . . . ?

HAVE YOU MET YOUR MATCH?

1. You and your fella are curled up all lovey-dovey watching a film on TV, when out of the blue he announces that he's enrolled for a French cookery course at the local Tech — him and 21 girls! D'you . . .

   c. join the car maintenance class with 16 dishy guys for company?

   a. tell him you'll look forward to sampling his first Quiche Lorraine?

   b. nip round to the Tech smartly and enrol for the same course?

   d. sulkily ask him why on earth he wants to learn to cook when he's got you?

2. It's an emergency!! You don't usually ring him at work but you feel you've no choice this time. The guy who answers the phone says cheerily, "Oh, hello, Sandie, hang on a sec and I'll get him." The only trouble is your name is Jane!! D'you . . .

   a. say nothing but wonder like mad who this Sandie could possibly be?

   d. demand to know immediately who this Sandie is?

   b. ask him casually (well, as casually as you can when you feel like killing him!) whether he's seen Sandie lately?

   c. tell him you only rang to say you couldn't make it that night as you'd just remembered you promised your brother's pal — you know, the tall, good-looking one — that you would give him a hand collecting for the youth club jumble sale?

3. It's Saturday afternoon and he's off playing football (as usual!). Your pal arrives to see if you fancy a trot around the shops and a coffee, and while you're both in the High Street you meet a couple of guys you know. You have such a good time laughing and joking with them that it's way past seven when you arrive home to find him waiting for you. What d'you do?

   d. You simply say that you went out shopping with a mate as you're certain he'd be insanely jealous if he knew you'd been drinking coffee with another fella!!

   a. You tell him truthfully what kept you but also tell him how pleased you are to see him!

   b. You don't say anything

unless he asks.

   c. You make the whole afternoon seem about a thousand times more exciting than it really was just to make him realise that football every single Saturday is a bit much!

4. On your birthday he arrives with a big square parcel wrapped in fancy white and silver paper.

Inside you find to your horror just about the most hideous frilly blouse you've ever seen. As he's all dressed up in his one-and-only suit and waiting for you to slip into the blouse so he can take you for a Chinese meal, you've got to think quickly. Do you . . .

c. say it's a lovely blouse but unfortunately you haven't a skirt to go with shocking pink candy stripes?

a. admire the blouse and thank him but tell him it really is much too small/large for you so you'll have to take it back?

d. feel that however awful it is he chose it for you and you'll have to wear it?

b. feel you have no alternative but to be totally honest and say you wouldn't be seen dead in it?

5. He's off for a month-long course at a college over 100 miles away. Before he goes he promises he'll come home each weekend to see you. But on his first weekend he says he can't afford to come home again as the train fare is too expensive. Do you . . .

a. know you'll miss him like mad but appreciate his financial problems and console yourself that another three weeks isn't a lifetime?

b. ask him what else he wants to spend his money on anyway if it isn't rushing home each weekend to see you?

d. burst into frantic sobs and tell him if you have to go even one more day, let alone three whole weeks, without seeing him, you just don't know what you'll do?

c. tell him that you'll write to him every single day?

6. You're watching "Top Of The Pops" with him and getting pretty cheesed off with his drooling every time he sees Debbie Harry. Do you . . .

b. say coolly, "It's wonderful what tricks they can do with photography these days?"

a. feel like smashing the TV set — but smile sweetly instead?

d. quiz him for hours as to whether he prefers her hair to yours, her figure to yours, or whether he would like you to dye your hair blonde?

c. drool over the next fanciable male singer who comes on?

Now tot up your scores and find out if you're perfect partners!

CONCLUSIONS

If you scored mostly a's: Does this fella of yours know how lucky he is to have such a lovable, understanding, easy-going girlfriend? Bet he does, 'cos he's probably as crazy over you as you are over him! You realise it's going to work out all hearts and roses for you both then enjoy the time you spend together every bit as much as the time you spend apart. Is this love? Well, you've certainly got all the ingredients . . . only time can tell!

Mostly b's: My goodness, you really think you own that guy of yours, don't you? You've got to learn to relax a little, give a little and learn to trust a little more. Try to have confidence in your own looks and personality and tell yourself you're just as interesting as other girls. Enjoy fellas and stop spusing as friends and stop worrying what everyone else thinks — everyone else isn't going out with him, are they? You can't turn every date into the biggest romance of the century but real love will turn up soon enough. So just wait and enjoy life — and see!

Mostly c's: Romance with laughter instead of tears seems to be your philosophy (most of the time, anyway). You realise that two coffees and a dance at the disco don't entitle you to know his every move 24 hours each day! You respect his right to have other friends and interests, too. Perhaps you've got a couple of older brothers around as you seem to have the knack of handling the male of the species. If he has a sense of humour, that fella of yours could be a guy-in-a-million, and finding out is going to be fun for both of you!

Mostly d's: Oh dear, what are we going to do with you? Or, more to the point, what is he going to do with you? OK, you claim he's the big romance of your life (sure you didn't say that about the last fella you went out with?). But really, all this bursting into tears is hardly going to make the fun run out of the year, is it? Don't blackmail him into doing what you want just by turning on the tears 'cos that's not a friendly thing to do, you know — he'll know you don't care without you clinging to his arm to prove it! Try to give your guy a little room to breathe 'cos otherwise he'll manage to shake you off for good!

The Way To A Guy's Heart . . . is through his stomach! Well, that's what they say, anyway! Here's a meal that'll certainly send your guy swooning! Invite your mate and her fella round, too — well, someone's got to wash the dishes!

(All amounts are enough for four people.)

SPAGHETTI BOLOGNAISE

1 lb. (400 g) minced beef
1 lb. (400 g) onions, peeled and sliced
½ lb. (200 g) mushrooms, wiped clean and chopped
1 (14 oz.) tin of peeled plum tomatoes
Small tin of tomato purée
½ pint stock (made up from a beef stock cube)
Salt and black pepper
1 clove of garlic, peeled and crushed
12 oz. (300 g) spaghetti
½ lb. (200 g) Cheddar cheese, grated

Make the sauce first. Brown the onion and mince in a large pan. Add mushrooms, tin of tomatoes (with their juice) and tomato purée. Stir well, then add stock. Season with salt, pepper and garlic. Cook over a gentle heat for one hour.

Fifteen minutes before the sauce is ready, start cooking the spaghetti. Half fill a pan with water, add salt and bring to the boil. Add spaghetti, lower it gently into pan, a little at a time, until it softens. Cook for twelve minutes, then drain through a colander.

Heap spaghetti on to plates, pour bolognaise sauce on top and sprinkle with grated cheese.

BISCUIT SUNDAE

1 packet lime jelly
1 small can evaporated milk
4-6 oz. (100-150 g) chocolate digestive biscuits.

Put the evaporated milk in the fridge to chill.

Make up the jelly with ¾ pint of water; cool, and leave until almost set.

When jelly is almost set, whisk the evaporated milk until really thick.

Slowly add the cooled jelly, whisking constantly, until the mixture itself is again really thick.

Crunch the chocolate biscuits (a quick way is to put them in a polythene bag and roll with a rolling-pin) then layer jelly and chocolate crumbs into tall glasses — also finishing with jelly. Chill and serve.

31

BE A BIG SOFTIE!

You will be when you snuggle up in our wonderful warm waistcoat!

MEASUREMENTS — To fit bust 81 (86, 91, 97) cm; 32 (34, 36, 38) ins. Full length — 43 (47, 49, 55) cm; 17 (18½, 19½, 21½) ins.

MATERIALS — Lister-Lee Tahiti — 8 (9, 9, 11) x 25 g balls. **Giselle** — 8 (9, 9, 11) x 20 g balls. Pair of 4½ mm (No. 7) needles; 3 x 4 mm (No. 8) needles (with points at both ends); 4 (4, 4, 5) buttons.

TENSION — 17 sts and 22 rows make 10 cm (4 ins) st-st using 4½ mm needles.

ABBREVIATIONS — K — knit; p — purl; sts — stitches; st-st — stocking-stitch; alt — alternate; foll — following; cont — continue; inc — increase; dec — decrease; rep — repeat; rem — remain(ing); beg — beginning; ws — wrong side; rs — right side; cm — centimetres; m1 — pick up loop lying between two needles and k into back of it; yfd — yarn forward; meas — measures; g-st — garter-stitch (k every row); skpo — slip one, knit one, pass slipped st over. Always cast on using the thumb method.

BACK

Using 4½ mm needles, cast on 65 (69, 74, 78) sts and work in st-st, inc one st at each end of 9th and every foll 8th row until 73 (77, 82, 86) sts. Cont on these sts until work meas 22 (24, 25, 31) cm, 8½ (9½, 10, 12) ins from beg, ending with a p row.

Shape Armholes —
Cast off 7 (7, 7, 8) sts at beg of next 2 rows. 59 (63, 68, 70) sts. Cont straight until work meas 19 (20, 21, 22) cm, 7½ (8, 8¼, 8½) ins, from beg of armhole shaping, ending with a p row.

Shape Shoulders and Neck —
Cast off 5 (6, 7, 7) sts at beg of next 2 rows.
Next row — Cast off 5 (6, 7, 7) sts, k 12 (12, 12, 13) sts, cast off 13 (13, 14, 14) sts, k to end. Cont on last set of sts as follows —
Next row — Cast off 5 (6, 7, 7) sts, p to end.
Next row — Cast off 6 sts, k to end. Cast off rem 7 (7, 7, 8) sts. With ws of work facing rejoin yarn to rem sts and cast off 6 sts, p to end. Cast off rem 7 (7, 7, 8) sts.

RIGHT FRONT

Using 4½ mm needles, cast on 3 sts.
1st row — K1, m1, k2.
2nd row — Cast on 2 sts, p to end.
3rd row — K 1, m1, k to end. Rep last 2 rows 6 (6, 6, 7) times more.

Next row — Cast on 2 (3, 4, 3) sts, p to end.
Next row — As 3rd.
Next row — Cast on 4 (5, 6, 6) sts, p to end.
Next row — As 3rd row. 33 (35, 37, 39) sts.
****Work 7 rows st-st. (1st row purl).
Inc one st at end of next and every foll 8th row until there are 37 (39, 41, 43) sts on needle.
Cont straight until work meas 19 (21, 23, 29) cm, 7½ (8¼, 9, 11½) ins, from beg, ending with a p row.
Shape Front —
1st row — K 1, skpo. Knit to end. Cont dec in this manner on next 4 (3, 3, 3) alt rows, then in the same way on every foll 4th row 8 (9, 9, 9) times. At the same time when side edge meas same as back to armhole, shape armhole as follows —
Next row — Cast off 7 (7, 7, 8) sts. Cont shaping at front edge only until 17 (19, 21, 22) sts rem. Cont straight until work meas same as back from beginning of armhole shaping to shoulder, ending on right side.
Shape Shoulder —
Cast off 5 (6, 7, 7) sts at beg of next and foll alt row. Work one row. Cast off rem sts.

LEFT FRONT

Using 4½ mm needles, cast on 3 sts.
1st row — K 2, m1, k 1.
2nd row — P to end, cast on 2 sts.
3rd row — K to last st, m1, k 1. Rep last 2 rows 6 (6, 6, 7) times more.
Next row — P to end, cast on 2 (3, 4, 3) sts.
Next row — As 3rd.
Next row — P to end, cast on 4 (5, 6, 6) sts.
Next row — As 3rd row — 33 (35, 37, 39) sts.
Now work as right front from **, reversing all shaping and working k 2 tog at front edge instead of skpo.

BACK NECK BORDER

With right side facing and using 4 mm needles, pick up and k 31 (31, 32, 32) sts across back of neck.

Continued on page **50**

I Sent A Letter...

SO, I SAID TO HIM, "LISTEN, PETER, IF YOU . . ." OH, HI, JOHN. DID YOU WANT ME?

YES, I—ER, HAVE YOU FINISHED TYPING THESE REPORTS FOR MR LEARY, SHIRLEY? HE'S BEEN MUTTERING ABOUT THEM ALL AFTERNOON.

YES, HERE THEY ARE. I JUST FINISHED THEM TWO MINUTES AGO. OK?

THANKS, SHIRL. UM, I WAS— OH, IT DOESN'T MATTER NOW.

ANYWAY, THERE WOULDN'T BE ANY POINT—SHE'S GOT LOADS OF BOYFRIENDS. AND SHE WOULDN'T WANT A SHY GUY LIKE ME WHEN SHE COULD HAVE ANY FELLA SHE WANTS.

AS I WAS SAYING, PAULA, I REALLY LET HIM HAVE IT—AND HE DESERVED IT, TOO, THE RAT. HE CAME ROUND TO APOLOGISE THIS MORNING AND ASKED FOR ANOTHER DATE, SO I TOLD HIM I'D THINK IT OVER . . .

IT'S NO GOOD, I'LL NEVER DO IT. I JUST HAVEN'T GOT THE COURAGE TO ASK HER OUT.

BUT FROM WHAT SHE WAS SAYING, IT SOUNDS LIKE SHE'S SPLITTING UP WITH HER PRESENT GUY. IF I COULD ONLY PLUCK UP THE COURAGE TO ASK HER, MAYBE I'D GET JUST ONE DATE . . .

IT'S NOT FAIR! WHY DO I HAVE TO FALL FOR A GIRL I CAN'T EVEN TALK TO? SHE JUST HAS TO SMILE AT ME, AND I LOSE ALL MY NERVE. SHE MAKES ME FEEL WEAK AT THE KNEES!

IT COULD ALL BE SO PERFECT IF I COULD JUST GET THROUGH TO HER. SHE'S SUCH A FUN PERSON, I CAN'T HELP LOVING HER. BUT SHE COULD LEARN TO LOVE ME TOO. I KNOW SHE COULD, IF ONLY I COULD TAKE THAT FIRST STEP . . .

Later . . .

HEY, THERE SHE IS—AND SHE'S ALONE, FOR A CHANGE! THAT'S A BIT OF LUCK—I KNOW SHE LIVES IN MY DIRECTION. IF WE CAN BE ALONE TOGETHER FOR A FEW MINUTES, SURELY I'LL BE ABLE TO FIND THE COURAGE TO ASK HER OUT . . .

But then . . .

HEY, SHIRLEY! LONG TIME NO SEE, EH? CLIMB IN AND I'LL DRIVE YOU HOME.

DAVE! WHERE'VE YOU BEEN HIDING?

WELL, THAT RUINED THAT IDEA. BLAST! IF ONLY I COULD GET HER ALONE, TELL HER HOW I FEEL, I'M SURE SHE'D LISTEN . . .

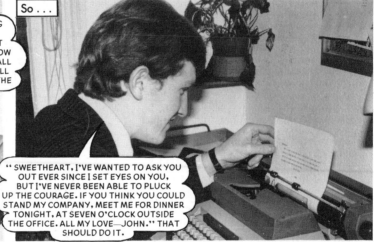

WORSE LUCK! I'VE FANCIED JOHN FOR MONTHS EVER SINCE I STARTED HERE. BUT I DON'T THINK HE EVEN KNOWS I EXIST . . .

HEY, WHAT'S THIS? I DON'T BELIEVE IT—IT'S LIKE A DREAM COME TRUE. IT'S A LETTER FROM JOHN AND HE'S ASKING ME FOR A DATE. I NEVER REALISED HE WAS SO SHY. OH, I CAN HARDLY WAIT FOR TONIGHT.

So, that evening . . .

I WISH HE'D HURRY UP—IT MUST BE SEVEN BY NOW. I HOPE HE ISN'T PLAYING A JOKE ON ME. BUT NO, JOHN WOULDN'T DO SOMETHING LIKE THAT . . .

Just then . . .

THERE SHE IS! BUT WAIT A MINUTE—THAT ISN'T SHIRLEY. IT'S THAT PRETTY GIRL FROM ACCOUNTS—DIANE. SHE MUST BE WAITING FOR SOMEONE ELSE WHICH MEANS SHIRLEY HASN'T TURNED UP, AFTER ALL . . .

But . . .

HELLO, JOHN. I WAS BEGINNING TO THINK YOU WEREN'T GOING TO TURN UP. SILLY OLD ME, BUT YOU KNOW HOW IT IS. I'VE BEEN DREAMING ABOUT THIS FOR SO LONG . . .

YEAH, I KNOW WHAT YOU MEAN.

SHE MUST'VE GOT HOLD OF THE MESSAGE SOMEHOW, AND THOUGHT IT WAS MEANT FOR HER. I CAN'T TELL HER IT'S ALL A MISTAKE. FROM THE LOOK ON HER FACE, SHE FANCIES ME AS MUCH AS I FANCY SHIRLEY. I'LL HAVE TO GO THROUGH WITH IT . . .

So . . .

MM, THIS IS DELICIOUS, JOHN. I'M SURE IT'S THE NICEST MEAL I'VE EVER HAD.

I'M GLAD YOU'RE ENJOYING IT.

I THOUGHT TONIGHT WAS GOING TO BE AWFUL, BUT IT ISN'T. DIANE'S REALLY GREAT FUN. IF I WASN'T SO CRAZY ABOUT SHIRLEY I COULD EASILY FALL FOR HER.

And, after they'd finished their meal.

WHAT DO YOU WANT TO DO NOW, THEN, DI? ANYTHING SPECIAL?

BEING WITH YOU MAKES ANYTHING SEEM SPECIAL. LET'S GO SOMEWHERE QUIET. I KNOW THIS LOVELY LITTLE PARK WHICH ISN'T TOO FAR AWAY.

ISN'T IT QUIET AND ROMANTIC HERE? YOU'D NEVER THINK WE WERE IN THE MIDDLE OF A CITY. I OFTEN COME HERE AFTER WORK, BUT HAVING YOU HERE WITH ME MAKES IT PERFECT . . .

I'M GLAD, DI. I LIKE IT, TOO.

I THOUGHT I WAS IMAGINING THINGS WHEN I SAW YOUR NOTE. TELL ME, JOHN, HOW DID YOU KNOW I WAS GOING TO BE TAKING SHIRLEY'S PLACE FOR A FEW DAYS?

I—ER . . . LISTEN, DI, I THINK I'D BETTER TELL YOU SOMETHING.

YOU SEE, THAT NOTE WASN'T REALLY MEANT FOR YOU. IT WAS FOR SHIRLEY. I THOUGHT I WAS IN LOVE WITH HER BUT MAYBE I WAS WRONG.

WHAT DO YOU MEAN, JOHN?

I WASN'T GOING TO TELL YOU, BUT I'VE ENJOYED TONIGHT SO MUCH, I'D LIKE US TO GO OUT AGAIN— AND I DON'T WANT TO DO THAT UNDER FALSE PRETENCES. Y'SEE, I KNOW NOW THAT I'M NOT IN LOVE WITH SHIRLEY.

I FEEL SO GUILTY ABOUT NOT TELLING YOU THE TRUTH RIGHT AT THE START. WILL YOU FORGIVE ME AND LET ME TAKE YOU OUT AGAIN? PLEASE?

LET ME TELL YOU A COUPLE OF THINGS. FIRST, YOU'RE A REAL HORROR AND YOU DON'T DESERVE ME—

—AND SECOND, I LOVE YOU ANYWAY! AND NOW THAT I'VE GOT YOU AT LAST, YOU DON'T HONESTLY THINK I'M GOING TO LET YOU GO, DO YOU? OF COURSE YOU CAN TAKE ME OUT AGAIN— TOMORROW, AND THE DAY AFTER, AND THE DAY AFTER THAT . . .

And so they sealed the deal with a kiss.

THE END

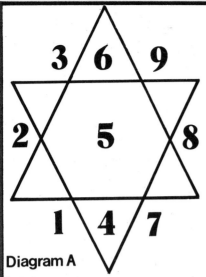

Diagram A

What's your number?

WANT a fun way of finding out what that new guy is *really* like? All you have to do is find out his birthdate — and from there you can discover all the secrets of his character.

The system was first worked out 2600 years ago in Greece — but it still works today!

Here's what you do —
Look at the double triangle (diagram A). You'll see that all the numbers between 1 and 9 have their own special place on the triangle. Draw a double triangle for yourself and position the numbers of **your** birthdate round it.

Here's an example. Say your date of birth is April 21, 1964 — the figures you'd have to distribute would be 21/4/1964 (the system doesn't use noughts, so if there are any noughts in your birthdate just ignore them).

In our example the finished diagram would look like this.

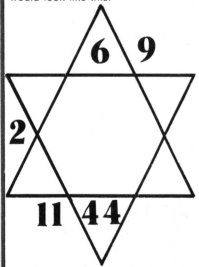

That's the hardest bit! Now all you have to do is look at the list below and find out what the numbers mean.

Single One (1) You've got a gift with words and find it easy to start conversations with new friends.

Two Ones (11) You're lucky — you can see both sides of a situation, so you don't always think *your* view is the right one!

Three Ones (111) This shows you've got writing talent — you can explain things much easier on paper than when you're speaking.

Four or more Ones (1111) You're very energetic and sometimes find it difficult to relax. You can be exhausting company sometimes!

Single Two (2) You're very quick to spot people who're trying to fool you, or anyone else. You're good at summing up other people, too, and it doesn't take you long to form an opinion about them.

Two Twos (22) You're a very sensitive person and can be hurt easily. Try not to be too touchy.

Three or more Twos (222) Watch your temper! You get frustrated easily, especially with other people and you're quick to show it!

Single Three (3) This points to a creative imagination and you can usually come up with the solution to other people's problems.

Two Threes (33) You don't like to follow what everyone else is doing — you'd rather come up with ideas of your own.

Three Threes (333) Make sure you don't get too self-centred — it'll put people off you!

Single Four (4) You're a practical, down-to-earth person, and you've got a gift for getting other people to do what you want.

Two Fours (44) An excellent organising ability is shown here.

Three Fours (444) You're very good with your hands — sewing, knitting, woodwork, painting and so on.

Single Five (5) This is one of the most important numbers in the chart. You're the kind of person who spurs other people on, and makes them realise their full capabilities.

Two Fives (55) You're a very strong character and other people could resent the way you try to shove them around.

Three Fives (555) Your family and friends may think you're a bit bossy, but you can be very persuasive, and you always manage to get your own way.

One Six (6) You're a home lover, and are happiest with the company of your family.

Two Sixes (66) The main problem you've got is you worry too much about other members of the family. Think of yourself first sometimes.

Three Sixes (666) You're a bit possessive about people you're close to and may tend to cling on to them too much.

Single Seven (7) You're inclined to worry too much, and most of your problems are caused by you being over-anxious.

Two Sevens (77) Other people bring their problems to you 'cos you're understanding and they know you'll do your best to help.

Three Sevens (777) Superstitious, that's you! You're interested in astrology, palm-reading — everything connected with the unknown, in fact!

Single Eight (8) You're a tidy, methodical person and like life to be pleasant and easy-going. With you around, it usually is!

Two Eights (88) You're very logical and like to work things out for yourself, rather than have them explained to you.

Three Eights (888) Success'll be yours! You work very hard to get what you want and the results are usually dramatic!

Single Nine (9) Everyone born in this century has at least one nine! This century'll allow creative people to make the most of their gifts.

Two Nines (99) You're a quick thinker and can be very quick at sorting out problems.

Three Nines (999) You've got a very quick, agile brain, but you'll have to make sure you use it properly.

FEELING FRUITY

Add a little zing to your life with these tutti-frutti recipes!

CITRUS CREAM

Ingredients
25 g butter
40 g caster sugar
25 g cornflour
284 ml milk
1 x 170 g can evaporated milk
Rind and juice from one lemon
1 egg, beaten
2 oranges, peeled and chopped

Place all ingredients, except oranges, in a pan. Heat, stirring continuously until the mixture thickens – this should take 3-4 minutes. Cool slightly, then half fill four individual glasses with the mixture. Place most of the chopped oranges over this and top with the remaining mixture.

Decorate with oranges, chill for an hour, then serve.

GRAPEFRUIT AND MELON REFRESHER

Ingredients
1 small ripe melon
1 grapefruit, peeled and segmented
2 tablespoonfuls lime juice
50 g caster sugar

Halve the melon and remove the seeds. Peel the melon halves and cut the flesh into cubes. Place in a large dish with the grapefruit segments, lime juice and sugar. Chill in the fridge for an hour, then serve in wine glasses.

FRUIT BRULÉE

Ingredients
1 dessertspoonful custard powder
1 dessertspoonful sugar
150 ml milk
350 g grapes, halved and seeded
150 ml fresh double cream
25 g brown sugar
25 g flaked almonds

Blend custard powder and sugar with a little milk. Heat remaining milk until almost boiling and pour over custard. Stir and return to pan. Heat, stirring until the custard thickens. Leave to cool. Place grapes in a shallow heatproof dish and pour cool custard over them.
Whip cream until thick and spread over fruit and custard. Chill thoroughly. Sprinkle with brown sugar and flaked almonds. Place under a preheated grill for 3-5 minutes and serve immediately.

All amounts given are enough for four people.

39

Roll up, roll up, for our...
PARTY PIECES

You'll never be lost in the crowd with one of these fantastic hairdos!

GOT a party coming up? Want to do something special to your hair, but you haven't a clue what? Then have a glance at these super styles, 'cos we've chosen something to suit almost every length and type of hair. Your friendly local hairdresser should be able to copy your fave — just show him or her the photo and you'll be halfway to being a real party smarty!

Head start

Here, the model's fine, mid-length hair was smoothly rolled up and back, with the front section curving down over her forehead to soften the look. It was designed by Ray of Sissors, London.

Eye-catcher

That's this style for layered, jaw-length hair. It was cut in a geometric bob to give a good, strong shape, then gently permed to give it a lively, bouncy look. He can run his fingers through this one and it'll still look great!
Cut by Ted at Sissors.

Wave hello...

. . . to a teasing style for longish hair. The loopy fringe draws attention to what your eyes're trying to say!
Irvine Rusk conditioned the hair with Clynol's Care Vitaliser then blow-dried it, the back downwards and the front forwards. It was then neatly rolled over a brush and pinned

Cascade

If you've got hair as long, wavy and thick as this girl we bet it drives you mad trying to keep it looking good! But doesn't this style look stunning? It's easy, too – the top sections of hair are simply rolled up from a centre parting and fixed with combs.
As well as looking really stylish, it holds your hair in place and takes away some of the width – so stopping your mop from looking too wild 'n' woolly! We've got Irvine Rusk to thank for this, and his salons are to be found in Glasgow, Hamilton, Clarkston and

Ice queen

Look as if you want to be alone – and you certainly won't be! This sophisticated style works best on straight, jaw-length hair. Irvine Rusk smoothed the hair up, moulded it into a curvy shape over the ears, and swept the front hair almost horizontally across the forehead. Then it was fixed in

Veiled secret

The Hair Now Group of Welwyn Garden City designed this mysterious style for girls with mid-length hair. After being sectioned off from the crown and plaited horizontally, a fine veil of hair is drawn down across the forehead.

But, of course, if you don't want to hide, the style would look just as good without the veil.

Sleek lights

Short hair needn't look at all boyish – this thick, layered cut shows off glossy, pretty-coloured hair beautifully. Amina at Michaeljohn of London produced this one, using vegetable colour to add richness to the hair as well as conditioning it.

Roll over

Another roll is softened by pulling out a lightly-crimped veil of hair to fall across the face. This style was produced by the Harold Kramer Group of Glasgow. Again, if you think the veil would annoy you, it looks equally good without – or simply with some tendrils pulled out around the nape of the neck.

Flirty forties

This is an updated Forties' look – softer and easier to wear than the original. Clynol's UniPerm was used by Albert Evansky of London to give plenty of bouncing body in the front and crown hair, while the sides and back were straightened with a blow-dryer and smoothed under.

Wave goodbye...

. . . to straight hair and plunge into these natural-looking waves! Malcolm of the Saks Group in the North-East designed this soft, easy-care style for shoulder-length layered hair, using Clynol's Waves ammonia-free permanent waving lotion.

And to cap it all...

This style shows off healthy, glossy hair to perfection with its curvy layered fringe. Designed by Jane of the Graham Webb Group for Inter coiffure (Great Britain), it gives shape and body to hair that tends to be a little on the thin side. And it's so easy to look after – it practically shakes into place!

GET THE PICTURE?

Hollywood, 1922—the fabulous city where unknowns become stars overnight. And other unknowns just hang around . . . still being unknown.

OH DEAR! WHO WOULD RECOGNISE LADY BELINDA TOTWELL OF TOTWELL TOWERS NOW? WASHING DISHES IN WHAT THE NATIVES OF THIS COUNTRY REFER TO AS A THIRD RATE JOINT?

COME ON, GET THOSE DISHES MOVIN'! THERE'RE FOLKS OUT HERE WHO WANNA EAT!

AND TO THINK I CAME OUT HERE IN THE HOPE OF BECOMING A STAR IN MOTION PICTURES, PAYING OFF DADDY'S GAMBLING DEBTS AND SAVING TOTWELL TOWERS! WHAT A FOOL I WAS!

I'VE MADE SUCH A MESS OF THINGS. OH, HOW I WISH I COULD BE LIKE SLAPSTICK SALLY SCHWARTZ, AMERICA'S SWEETHEART. BRAVE . . .

. . . SO FUNNY . . .

. . . AND BE ABLE TO STAR IN EVERY PICTURE WITH MY IDOL, RAYMOND FLAMENCO! BUT IT'S NO USE, I COULD NEVER BE LIKE HER . . .

But Belinda wouldn't give up. And next day found her heading in the same direction as always . . .

PARAGON PICTURES INC
APPLICANTS FOR WORK

ARE YOU KIDDIN'? I NEED THAT JOB YOU'RE OFFERIN' LIKE I NEED A BROKEN LEG!

HOW DIFFERENT IT COULD'VE BEEN, IF ONLY DEAR BEN HAD COME BACK TO CLAIM ME! EVEN IF HE WAS ONLY THE GARDENER'S SON, HE DID SWEAR ETERNAL LOVE TO ME BEFORE HE RAN AWAY TO SEA.

AND DON'T LOOK AT ME, NEITHER! YOU TALKED MY GIRLFRIEND INTO TAKING IT A WHILE BACK—AND SHE DID END UP WITH A BROKEN LEG!

HE WAS BUT TWELVE AT THE TIME, AND I ONLY EIGHT, BUT A PROMISE IS A PROMISE—AND HE SHOULD HAVE KEPT IT!

LITTLE LADY, I'M A DIRECTOR. WHAT WOULD YOU SAY TO THE CHANCE OF A HUNDRED DOLLARS A DAY FOR WORKING ALONGSIDE SLAPSTICK SALLY SCHWARTZ, AMERICA'S SWEETHEART?

BUT MISS SCHWARTZ IS MY IDOL—AND A HUNDRED DOLLARS A DAY IS A FORTUNE! FOR A CHANCE LIKE THAT I'D WRESTLE WITH LIONS!

BELIEVE ME, HONEY— THAT'S JUST WHAT YOU MIGHT FIND YOURSELF DOING!

Later . . .

THERE SHE IS—THE REAL SALLY SCHWARTZ! AND SHE'S EVEN MORE LOVELY OFF THE SCREEN THAN ON.

OK, MISS SCHWARTZ—TIME TO ROLL 'EM. ER, THAT IS . . . IF YOU DON'T MIND.

BUT I CAN'T HELP WONDERING WHAT'S TO BE MY PART IN THIS PICTURE . . .

RIGHT—CU—!

SEE YOU, HONEY. I NEVER DID CARE FOR PIE.

OK, MISS—IT'S YOUR BIG CHANCE NOW.

MY BIG CHANCE! AND IF I SUCCEED PERHAPS I TOO WILL BECOME A STAR AND SAVE TOTWELL TOWERS FROM BEING SOLD . . .

But then . . . Splat!

EE-E-EEK!

And then the cameras turned towards Sally again . . .

LIKE I SAID, I NEVER DID CARE FOR PIE. I LEAVE THAT PART TO HUNDRED-DOLLAR-A-DAY STAND-INS. AND, SWEETIE, I'M GONNA MAKE SURE YOU EARN EVERY CENT OF THAT MONEY!

YOU . . . YOU NEED A LESSON IN MANNERS! YOU MAY BE CALLED AMERICA'S SWEETHEART, BUT IN MY OPINION YOU'RE NOTHING BUT A . . .

HEY, COOL DOWN! IT DOESN'T PAY TO CROSS MISS CHARM THERE. HER CONTRACT SAYS SHE CAN FIRE ANYBODY SHE DOESN'T LIKE. AND THAT INCLUDES THE DIRECTOR —AND ME!

RAYMOND FLAMENCO— THE LATIN LOVER!

AT YOUR SERVICE—BUT ACTUALLY I'M AS BRITISH AS YOU ARE. HOWEVER, DON'T LET ON—IT COULD RUIN ME IN MOVIES!

RAYMOND HONEY, WOULD YOU COME OVER ONE TEENY WEENY MINUTE AND DISCUSS THE NEXT SCENE WITH ME?

COMING, MY DEAR.

I'D BETTER GO—BUT WATCH YOUR STEP, LOVE—'COS IF SALLY GETS IT INTO HER MEAN LITTLE HEAD THAT I LIKE YOU, SHE'S CAPABLE OF ANYTHING!

And so the filming went on . . .

OK—CUT! HOLD THE HOUSE RIGHT THERE, AND BRING ON THE STAND-IN!

... with things getting worse ...

NOW REMEMBER, WHATEVER YOU DO, BELINDA BABY—DON'T TAKE YOUR FEET OFF THAT CHALKLINE. OTHERWISE YOU COULD GET HURT. OK—ACTION!

B-BUT ... THERE ISN'T A CHALKLINE!

... and worse!

OW—MY ARM!

LOOK OUT! FOR HEAVENS' SAKE—IT NEARLY HAD HER!

YOU KNOW, I RECKON YOU OUGHT TO GET RID OF THAT GIRL. THE KID'S NO TROUPER!

SHE'S RIGHT, THERE IS NO CHALK MARK. IT'S BEEN RUBBED OUT!

AMERICA'S SWEETHEART DID THAT—I'LL BET MY LAST QUID ON IT. LOOK, BELINDA—YOU'D BETTER GET OUT OF HERE BEFORE YOU GET REALLY HURT.

NO, I WON'T GIVE HER THAT SATISFACTION. AND BESIDES, I DO RATHER NEED THE MONEY!

DON'T WE ALL? I'VE GOT A MANSION IN BEVERLEY HILLS TO SUPPORT! BUT I DO THINK YOU'D BE WISE TO ... HEY, WHAT'S THAT?

OH, NOTHING—JUST HALF A PENNY. THE OTHER HALF BELONGS TO A BOY I USED TO KNOW ... B-BUT I DON'T LIKE TO TALK ABOUT IT.

Later ...

THAT WAS GREAT, MISS SCHWARTZ, BUT THE STAND-IN CAN TAKE OVER, NOW.

NOW REMEMBER, WHEN YOU STEP FORWARD THE PLANKS'LL GIVE WAY UNDERFOOT—BUT AS LONG AS YOU KEEP HOLDING THE ROPE YOU'LL BE ABLE TO STOP YOURSELF FALLING. OK?

I ... ER ... THINK SO.

THERE ARE TIMES ... WHEN I WONDER ... IF KEEPING TOTWELL TOWERS IN THE FAMILY ... IS WORTH ALL THIS TROUBLE.

AND THIS IS ONE OF THEM! THE ROPE—IT'S SNAPPED, TOO!

AAAAGH!

GOOD GRIEF, THAT ROPE WASN'T SUPPOSED TO BREAK!

STRIKES ME YOU EMPLOY SOME PRETTY CRUMMY PROP MEN AROUND HERE. NOW WHERE'S RAYMOND GONE? I COULD DO WITH A CUP OF COFFEE.

BELINDA—ARE YOU ALL RIGHT?

I- I THINK SO, RAYMOND. BUT WHAT HAPPENED ... OR CAN I GUESS?

THE ROPE WAS HALF CUT THROUGH. AMERICA'S SWEETHEART STRIKES AGAIN! IT'S NO GOOD, I'VE HAD IT UP TO HERE WITH THAT DAME. I'M QUITTING!

NOT WITHOUT ME, YOU DON'T. BUT FIRST I'M GOING TO GIVE SALLY SCHWARTZ THE SPANKING OF HER LIFE—AND THEN I'M GOING TO TELL THE TRUTH ABOUT HER TO EVERY PAPER IN THE STATES!

AND YOU'LL DO ALL THIS FOR ME, AFTER KNOWING ME FOR ONLY A FEW HOURS? HOW VERY CHIVALROUS! BUT PRETTY SILLY TOO—'COS ALL IT'LL DO IS WRECK YOUR CAREERS AS WELL AS MINE! NO, THERE'S GOT TO BE A BETTER WAY.

And that night, at the Beverley Hills mansion of Raymond Flamenco, they tried hard to think of one. But . . .

PIRANHAS IN SALLY'S SWIMMING POOL? NO— WHAT'VE THE PIRANHAS DONE TO DESERVE IT?

HOW'S ABOUT . . . NO. WE THOUGHT OF THAT, HOURS AGO. HECK, THIS IS JUST PLAIN HOPELESS. LET'S FACE IT, SLAPSTICK SALLY SCHWARTZ HAS GOT US LICKED!

HANG ON—I THINK I'VE THE ANSWER TO OUR PROBLEMS. LOOK, THIS IS MISS SCHWARTZ'S CONTRACT, AND . . .

FORGET IT—THAT THING'S WATERTIGHT. DRAWN UP BY THE BEST LAWYERS ON THE WEST COAST.

SHE'S GOT THE RIGHT TO FIRE EVERYBODY IN SIGHT, BUT NOBODY CAN FIRE HER. NO, SHE'S COVERED EVERYTHING!

REALLY? THEN WHY DOESN'T IT SAY HERE THAT SHE MUST ALWAYS HAVE A STAND-IN TO DO ANYTHING DIFFICULT OR DANGEROUS? BECAUSE, BELIEVE ME, IT DOESN'T!

BUT . . . BUT . . . THAT'S JUST WHAT WE NEED. BELINDA, YOU'RE FANTASTIC! COME ON, WE'VE GOT WORK TO DO. AMERICA'S SWEETHEART'S IN FOR THE SURPRISE OF HER LIFE!

So, next morning, on the set . . .

HEY, WHY DON'T YOU SAY "CUT" AND LET MY STAND-IN TAKE OVER THE MOLASSES SHOWER? I HEAR IT'S AWFUL GOOD FOR THE COMPLEXION, SWEETIE!

STAND-IN, MISS SCHWARTZ? BUT YOU MUST BE MISTAKEN. THERE'S NO MENTION OF YOU HAVING ONE IN YOUR CONTRACT.

SO FROM HERE ON IN, THERE JUST AIN'T GONNA BE ONE! SEE WHAT I MEAN?

E-E-E-EK!

HERE, LOOK IN THE CONTRACT YOURSELF. AND WHILE YOU DO, WE'LL TAKE YOU ACROSS TO THE OTHER SET. IS IT ALL READY, GENTLEMEN?

READY AND RARIN' TO GO! PLACES, EVERYBODY, FOR THE RUNAWAY LOCOMOTIVE SCENE—TAKE FOUR!

NOW YOU'RE NOT TO WORRY WHEN THE LOCOMOTIVE CROSSES THE BRIDGE AT EIGHTY MILES AN HOUR, JUMPS THE GAP AND LANDS ON THE OTHER SIDE, MISS SCHWARTZ. YOU SEE, YOU CAN'T FALL OFF—'COS YOU'LL BE SECURELY ROPED TO THE FRONT OF IT!

AND IT'LL MAKE A WONDERFUL SCENE—COMING AS IT DOES, RIGHT AFTER THE ONE WHERE YOU FIGHT THE OCTOPUS. OR DIDN'T WE TELL YOU ABOUT THAT?

YOU'RE BANANAS—THE WHOLE COTTON-PICKIN' LOT OF YOU! I'M NOT STICKING ROUND HERE TO GET KILLED. I QUIT!

YOU DID IT, BELINDA—YOU DID THE IMPOSSIBLE. I COULD KISS YOU FOR THAT . . . AND I WILL.

OH NO, YOU WON'T! FOR THAT, YOU NEED HER FIANCE'S PERMISSION, AND I'M NOT GIVING IT!

FIANCE? BUT YOU'VE NEVER EVEN ASKED ME IF I'D . . .

OH, BUT I DID— YEARS AGO. REMEMBER? LOOK—DON'T YOU RECOGNISE THE OTHER HALF OF YOUR PENNY?

BEN, IT CAN'T BE . . . IT JUST CAN'T BE . . . YOU?

But it was . . . and he was easily rich enough to buy Totwell Towers.

THE END

ARE YOU SWITCHED ON?

Try our tricky telly quiz and see if you pass our screen test!

Testing, Testing, 1
1. Who's this famous TV personality?
2. Which channel does she appear on?
3. On whose programme did she "show a leg"?

Cop This!
You should all be used to watching the detectives — so now's your chance to answer a few questions on your top telly 'tecs!
1. Which actor plays the part of Jim Rockford?
2. What's the screen name of the private eye who loves drawing cartoons?
3. Name the actor who plays the part of James Hazell.
4. Which tough character does Angie Dickinson play?
5. What's the dishy cop's favourite means of transport in "Chips"?

Best Foot Forward
1. What's the name of "Top Of The Pops'" resident dancers?
2. Name the dancers who provide the "naughty bits" on the "Kenny Everett Video Show."
3. What's the name of the dancers who left the "Kenny Everett Video Show" gang to form their own group?
4. What's the name of the lovely ladies who're seen every week on the "Little and Large Show"?
5. What star of "Give Us A Clue" used to be a top dancer?

Oldies, But Goldies
Now's your chance to take a stroll down memory lane with us and remember some of the great programmes of the past. We've missed out one word from all the titles — all you've got to do is fill it in.
1. Peyton -----.
2. The ------- Saga.
3. --------- Ward Ten.
4. Z ----.
5. Dixon Of ---- Green.
6. Ready, ------ Go!

News Flash
1. Which TV interviewer had a famous fight with an Emu?

A Question Of Sport!
There's always plenty of sport to watch on the telly — so here's your chance to find out just how much you know about it. On your marks, get set, go!
1. Which two famous tennis stars made a love-match by getting married?
2. Who introduces "World of Sport"?
3. Which English football player now plays for Real Madrid?
4. What sport do Giant Haystack, Big Daddy, Rollerball Rocco and Catweazel take part in?
5. "Pot Black" is a programme about which sport?
6. Which British athlete held world records in the 800 metres, the mile and the 1500 metres?
7. "Bully off" is a term used in which sport?

That's Odd
Which one in the following groups of people is the odd one out — and why?
1. Robin Day, Bamber Gascoigne, Trevor McDonald, Noel Edmonds.
2. Frankie Howerd, Dave Allan, Ronnie Barker, Ken Dodd.
3. Faith Brown, Mike Yarwood, Paul Daniels, Paul Melba.
4. Tom Baker, Jon Pertwee, Patrick Troughton, Spike Milligan.
5. Dave Lee Travis, Pete Powell, David Hamilton, Simon Bates.

News Flash
2. What's the name of the scoreboard in "Family Favourites"?

Testing, Testing, 2
1. What's this lovely lady's name?
2. Which programme does she introduce?
3. What's the name of the famous dog that appears with her on the show?

Top Of The Props
Which famous telly people do you associate with these odd items?
1. A fez.
2. A pair of spectacles.
3. A rocking chair.
4. A tickling stick.
5. A didgereedoo.

Tasty Serials!
We all love those exciting serials on the box — so as a special treat, we'll ask you a few questions about your family favourites!
1. What's actor David Hunter's son's name in "Crossroads"?
2. What part does actress Doris Speed play in "Coronation Street"?
3. What part does dishy Patrick Duffy play in "Dallas"?
4. What's the name of the butler in "Soap"?

The Generation Game!

Here's a game for all the family!

All you've got to do is match up the stars in these boxes with their famous fathers or mothers.

1

2

3

4

5

6

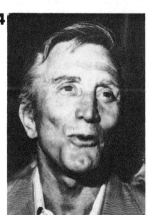

7

8

Testing, Testing, 3

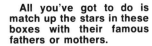

1. What's this actress's name in real life?
2. What's the name of her hen-pecked husband on television?
3. What's the surname of their next-door neighbours in the programme?

★★★★★★★

News Flash!

3. In what programme does Swiftnick appear?

★★★★★★★

Answers

News Flash
3. Dick Turpin.

Testing, Testing, 3
1. Yootha Joyce.
2. George.
3. The Fourmiles.

The Generation Game
Number 1 – Ryan O'Neal with his daughter, Number 2 – Tatum O'Neal. Number 4 – Kirk Douglas with his son, Number 6 – Michael Douglas. Number 7 – Harvey Smith with his son, Number 5 – Robert Smith. Number 8 – John Mills with his daughter, Number 3 – Hayley Mills.

Tasty Serials!
1. Chris.
2. Annie Walker.
3. Bobby Ewing.
4. Benson.

Top of the Props!
1. Tommy Cooper.
2. Eric Morecambe.
3. Val Doonican.
4. Ken Dodd.
5. Rolf Harris.

Testing, Testing, 2
1. Sally James.
2. "Tiswas."
3. Spit.

News Flash
2. Mr Babbage.

5. David Hamilton – the others are all DJ's on Radio One.
4. Spike Milligan – the rest all played the part of Doctor Who.
3. Paul Daniels – the rest are impersonators.
2. Dave Allen – the others rest wear glasses.

That's Odd
1. Noel Edmonds – the rest wear glasses.

7. Hockey.
6. Sebastian Coe.
5. Snooker.
4. Wrestling.
3. Laurie Cunningham.
2. Dickie Davis.

A Question Of Sport
1. John Lloyd and Chris Evert.

News Flash
1. Michael Parkinson.

6. Steady.
5. Dock.
4. Cars.
3. Emergency.
2. Forsyte.
1. Place.

Oldies, But Goldies
5. Lionel Blair.
4. Foxy Feelings.
3. Sponooch.
2. Hot Gossip.
1. Legs and Co.

Best Foot Forward
5. Motorbikes.
4. Pepper Anderson.
3. Nicholas Ball.
2. Eddie Shoestring.
1. James Garner.

Cop This!
3. "The Morecambe and Wise Show."
2. BBC.
1. Angela Rippon.

Testing, Testing, 1

No-one cared whether I lived or died and I felt so miserable and alone. I didn't think life could get any worse — then I discovered I was pregnant . . .

MY LIFE WAS IN RUINS

THE baby was wearing a pink woollen bonnet. One small hand curled on top of the rough blanket. I touched it with my finger, very gently, then tucked it back under the cover. She never stirred.

Every morning as I walked down that road to the supermarket where I worked, I saw the baby in the pram by the green front door. Every morning I paused for a few seconds and looked at her.

Why did they put her out there so early, I wondered. Was it to get her out of the way?

"I wouldn't push you out here early in the morning, not if you were mine," I muttered. But she wasn't mine and it was with a heavy heart that I trudged down the road, trying in vain not to let the bitter memories overwhelm me . . .

My mum and dad had split up when I was seven and both had re-married. I stayed with Mum during the week and went to Dad some weekends and holidays, but I didn't feel as if I belonged at either house. No-one really wanted me, no-one seemed to care what happened to me. So I started staying out late at night and got in with a rough crowd at school. Why should I bother when no-one else did?

My head was spinning

One evening I overheard Mum complaining about me to Jim, her new husband, going on about what a problem I was. All he did was grunt in agreement — he didn't want to know either.

That did it — I stormed out of the house and headed for the pub where I knew the gang would be. One drink lead to another and before I knew it I was quite tipsy.

Nick, the boy I was sort of going out with, said he'd see me home, and I was feeling so light-headed I was glad of his offer. At least he seemed to like me, I thought.

When the fresh air hit me my head began to spin, and when Nick took me in his arms and kissed me, I felt all my troubles floating away. I suppose that's why I didn't stop him when his kisses became more insistent. But when he tried to go further, I pulled back a bit.

"What's up?" he mumbled. "Don't tell me you're scared!"

By this time I was too tired and drunk to try to fight him off. Besides, I knew Mum didn't approve of him, and in my crazy way of thinking right then this seemed to be a way of hitting back at her . . .

I never once thought about getting pregnant. I was quite confident that you never did,

the first time. That's how naive I was, in spite of my show of self-confidence.

How wrong I was! I'd been worried for a couple of weeks and when I started being sick in the mornings my worst fears were confirmed.

I nearly went frantic — after all, I wasn't sixteen for another couple of months — I couldn't even leave school.

I couldn't tell Mum. Things weren't too good between her and Jim these days. They always seemed to be arguing, and she had less and less time for me.

But in the end I had to tell her. I mean, it's not something you can hide for ever. She just went wild and slapped my face — it was no more than she'd expected, she shouted. We had a terrible row and in the end I slammed out of the house.

I wandered along by the canal and, looking at the water, I thought, suppose I throw myself in — that'd solve everything. But the thought of that cold, dark water closing over my head and filling my eyes and mouth made me shudder. I couldn't — I just couldn't do that.

I hadn't seen much of Nick since that night after the pub. I'd kept away from the gang, preferring to mooch around on my own.

I found myself reluctant to tell him — what could he do anyway? I was too young to get married, even if I'd wanted to, which I didn't.

And then I heard that the police had caught Nick in a stolen car. This wasn't the first time that he'd been in trouble and they'd be sure to send him to Borstal this time.

I'd been to the doctor, and he'd arranged for a social worker to call and see me, and I really had no option but to go along with what she suggested: I'd go to a Mother and Baby Home in the country three weeks before the baby was due, and have it adopted from there.

"Then you can come back and start afresh," she said brightly.

Easy for her to say that, I thought sourly. Start afresh? Where? Doing what?

"I'll have a little talk with your mother," she went on. "I'm sure we can sort something out."

I'm sure we can't, I thought dismally. Mum had hardly spoken a word to me since she knew about the baby. And I was sick of hanging around in a place I wasn't wanted.

So that night I took the money that Mum kept under the clock on the mantelpiece, pushed my few belongings into a battered old suitcase and set off for London.

I must have walked for miles

that first day, but eventually I found a single room to rent that was fairly cheap — a rather dark, damp little attic right at the top of a shabby old house. But it was furnished — after a style.

Then I tramped around till I found a job, washing up in a Wimpy bar.

In a funny sort of way, I almost enjoyed those months in London. I was dreadfully lonely, of course, but I spent a lot of my spare time wandering all over London, exploring. I'd never been there before, and even in my condition it was quite exciting.

No friends

I hadn't any friends — I didn't want any friends. The only way I could cope with my problem was by trying to pretend it wasn't happening! I even wore chunky jumpers or loose shirts to disguise my shape, so that no-one would know.

I hadn't really worked out what I was going to do when it came to the time for me to have my baby. I reckoned I'd go to that Mother and Baby Home the social worker had suggested. But one night I woke up with a curious, niggling pain in my back.

Lying there, alone in the dark, I clasped my hands over my stomach. It couldn't be now — it was too soon! I shivered, and a feeling of sheer panic spread all through me. What on earth was I going to do?

I found myself wishing frantically that I was at home — even being nagged and told off would be better than lying here alone, not knowing what to do.

Clumsily I got out of bed and dragged my clothes on — I even brushed my hair. I gathered up a few things, pushed them into my shoulder-bag, and set out for the hospital near the supermarket.

It took me ages to get there. Once or twice, I thought I wouldn't make it, but at last I stumbled through the big iron gates, past the porter's room and into the Casualty Department.

There was one man sitting there waiting, reading a newspaper. I heard someone laugh, and saw a nurse disappear into one of the cubicles, so I followed her.

"I think — I — I'm having my baby — early," I gasped.

Things moved fast after that and in no time I found myself in bed, being examined by a doctor.

It's all a bit hazy, but I know they gave me an injection of some sort and several hours later my baby was born —

tiny and frail and premature, she was whisked away into an incubator.

I turned my face into the pillow and cried and cried. I just couldn't stop.

The social worker came to see me, and so did Mum. The baby was to be adopted as arranged. I agreed to everything. I felt numb inside. I wouldn't see the baby. I still wanted to pretend it hadn't happened.

When I left the hospital Mum came to take me home. But, if anything, living with Mum and Jim was even worse than before.

Mrs Williams, the social worker, got me a job in the supermarket, which was better than nothing. At least it kept me out of Mum's way during the day.

I tried to forget about the baby, shut it out of my mind, and I succeeded — till I started noticing the pram outside that house, and the baby in the pink woollen bonnet.

One day, a Sunday, I went for a walk, and found myself wandering down the street where the baby lived. The pram was there, and the child was asleep. She must've been out all day, I thought indignantly.

The road was quiet and deserted. I put out one finger and touched the soft, rounded cheek, and her eyelashes fluttered.

I looked up at the house — at the closed door, the blank windows. No-one stirred.

There was a brick wedged under one wheel — I pushed it aside with my foot and eased the pram out on to the pavement.

It felt so right somehow, pushing that pram. I went into the park and sat on a seat by the duck pond.

I'll take her back presently, I thought, but just for a little while I can pretend she's mine — pretend that I did keep her, didn't let her go to strangers. Hot tears stung my eyes — I felt so guilty, abandoning my little baby like that.

The baby stirred

I rocked the pram gently as the baby stirred, then tucked the blanket in carefully; and when she opened her eyes and yawned, I lifted her out very gently and cuddled her to me. She felt warm and comforting, her head resting on my shoulder, and I felt happier and more relaxed than I'd been for ages.

I was still sitting there like that when someone came and sat down on the seat beside me — a policewoman.

Continued Overleaf.

MY LIFE WAS IN RUINS

Continued From Previous Page.

"What a lovely baby," she said quietly. "Is she your sister?"

I shook my head.

"No — I — I'm just looking after her — for someone."

"Don't you think we'd better take her back then?" she asked gently. "Her mother's very upset. You didn't tell her you were taking her for a walk, did you?"

"She doesn't care — she just leaves her outside all the time," I said indignantly.

"Now what makes you think that? They love her very much. You can see how well she's looked after. She's clean and healthy and happy, isn't she?"

Tears

She was right, I had to admit it. Reluctantly I tucked her back into the pram, and the policewoman kept one hand firmly on the pram handle as I pushed it slowly back out of the park.

"I'll take her the rest of the way," she said, as a policeman appeared beside me. To my bewilderment I found myself being put in the back of a police car and driven to the station.

I was taken into a small room and another policewoman brought me a cup of tea, and sat down opposite me.

"Suppose you tell me all about it?" she suggested.

"I wouldn't have hurt her — the baby, I mean. I was going to take her back, honestly I was. I — I don't know why I did it." I burst into tears.

I had to tell them who I was and where I lived and every-thing. In the end they contacted Mrs Williams and Mum — Mrs Williams came round right away and she took me home. But I knew I couldn't stay there. Mum didn't want to know — and who could blame her? She was right really, I'd been nothing but worry and trouble to her, and I hadn't even tried to get on with her. It didn't stop me feeling very hurt and bitter though.

To my amazement it was my dad who finally came to the rescue. Mrs Williams had got in touch with him, and he was very angry that no-one had told him about me being pregnant and disappearing and every-thing.

"Poor Dawn, you've had a rough time," he said. "I'm taking you back with me now, love, and no arguments. You'll like living up there, it's in the country and I think I can get you a job on the farm up the road. Remember when you were little how you always said you'd like to work with animals?"

"What about — well, your — your wife?" I faltered at last.

"Emmie? She feels really bad about all this too, and she wants to make a go of it. Give her a chance, eh, Dawn? Meet her halfway?"

I wasn't too optimistic, I must say, but I hadn't much choice. I had nowhere else to go.

"Yes, I'll come with you, Dad," I said, managing a tremulous smile. Dad squeezed my hand. I knew I'd have to make an effort this time. I'd been lucky enough to get a second chance, and it was up to me to make it work out.

50

BE A BIG SOFTIE

Work 7 rows in g-st, dec 2 sts on 3rd and 7th rows. Cast off.

LOWER BACK BORDER
With right side facing and using 4 mm needles, pick up and k 65 (69, 74, 78) sts across lower edge of back. Work 7 rows g-st. Cast off.

RIGHT FRONT BORDER (including buttonholes)
With right side facing and using 3 x 4 mm needles, beg at lower side edge of front, pick up and k 29 (31, 33, 35) sts along side of slope to 3 cast-on sts, 17 (17, 17, 19) sts along front slope, 31 (33, 36, 47) sts along straight front edge and 48 (49, 49, 49) sts along shaped edge to shoulder. K 1 row. Cont in g-st and start to shape. On the following row inc 2 sts at lower point, 1 st at front corner and 1 st at beg of front shaping. K 1 row.

Next row — K 2 tog, work to point, inc 2 sts at point, k until there are 50 (52, 54, 58) sts on right-hand needle. M1, k 2 (3, 3, 3). *Yfd, k 2 tog, k 7 (7, 8, 8) sts, rep from * 2 (2, 2, 3) times, yfd, k 2 tog, k to end, working inc as before. K 1 row.

Next row — K inc as before. K 1 row. Cast off.

LEFT FRONT BORDER
With right side of work facing and using 3 x 4 mm needles and beginning at shoulder, pick up and k 48 (49, 49, 49) sts along shaped edge, 31 (33, 36, 47) sts along straight front edge, 17 (17, 17, 19) sts along front slope to centre of the 3 cast-on sts and 29 (31, 33, 35) sts along side of slope to side edge. K 1 row.

Continue in g-st and start to shape. On foll row inc one st at beg of front shaping, 1 st at front corner and 2 sts at lower point. K 1 row.

4th row — K 49 (50, 50, 50) sts, m1, k until 50 sts remain on left-hand needle, m1, k to point, inc 2 sts as before, k to last 2 sts, k 2 tog. K 1 row.

Next row — K, inc as before. K 1 row.
Cast off.

ARMHOLE BORDERS
Join shoulder seams. With right side of work facing and using 4 mm needles, pick up and k 69 (72, 75, 79) sts around armhole edge, omitting cast-off sts. Work 8 (8, 8, 9) rows g-st. Cast off.

TO MAKE UP
Sew ends of armhole borders to cast-off sts. Join side seams. Sew on buttons to match buttonholes. For a really luxurious effect lightly hand brush the finished garment.

SNACK HAPPY!

Feeling peckish? Well, these tasty snacks'll soon fill the gap!

SALMON DREAMS

Ingredients

16 slices of white bread
50 g unsalted butter
1 x 215 g canned salmon, drained
50 g cream cheese
1 tablespoonful grated Cheddar cheese
Salt and black pepper
1 egg
1 tablespoonful milk
Paprika
Fat for frying

Using a 5 to 7.5 cm (2 to 3 inch) scone cutter, cut 16 circles from the bread, and butter each circle. Remove any skin and bone from the salmon. Mash the flesh with a fork, then stir in the cream cheese and grated cheese. Season to taste with salt and pepper. Spread the mixture thickly on half the bread circles. Top with the remaining slices and press firmly together. Beat together with eggs and milk. Season with salt, pepper and paprika. Dip the sandwiches in the beaten egg mixture and fry in shallow, hot fat until crisp and golden. Drain on kitchen paper and serve hot.

Cinderella Gets Her Fella!

Once upon a time, in the Ellis household, the Wednesday morning peace was shattered by . . .

HEATHER, THEY'RE HERE! LOOK, OUR TICKETS FOR THE OPENING OF THE NEW DISCO. THEY'VE ARRIVED.

THAT'S FANTASTIC! I CAN HARDLY WAIT. THE BALL OF FIRE DISCO WON'T KNOW WHAT'S HIT IT WHEN WE WALK IN.

TWITS! THEY'VE SENT US THREE TICKETS AND WE ONLY ASKED FOR TWO.

MAYBE WE COULD GIVE IT TO ONE OF THE GIRLS AT WORK.

I DON'T SUPPOSE I COULD HAVE THE EXTRA TICKET, COULD I, IVY?

YOU! YOU MUST BE JOKING, CINDY. THIS ISN'T SOME SCHOOL DANCE WE'RE TALKING ABOUT. THIS IS A SPECIAL NIGHT OUT FOR MATURE, SOPHISTICATED, SLINKY PEOPLE—LIKE US!

NO, WAIT A MINUTE. LET HER HAVE THE TICKET IF SHE WANTS. HERE YOU ARE, LITTLE SISTER.

OH, THANKS. THANKS A MILLION, HEATHER!

BUT YOU DO REALISE THE OPENING NIGHT IS THURSDAY. THAT'S THE NIGHT YOU BABYSIT FOR MUM 'N' DAD!

WH- WHAT!? OH, NO . . .

C'MON, CINDY, OR YOU'LL BE LATE FOR SCHOOL.

THEY'RE ALWAYS ROTTEN TO ME, JUST 'COS I'M YOUNGER! IT'S NOT FAIR!

Miserably, Cindy told her mum about her problem . . .

I TELL YOU WHAT, I'LL ASK MRS PATERSON NEXT DOOR IF SHE CAN BABYSIT.

OH, MUM, WOULD YOU? THANKS!

But that night . . .

I'M SORRY, LOVE, BUT MR AND MRS PATERSON ARE GOING OUT TOMORROW NIGHT, SO YOU'LL HAVE TO BABYSIT AFTER ALL.

OH . . . I—I SEE . . .

From then on, all they talked about was the disco.

I'M GOING TO KNOCK 'EM FOR SIX TOMORROW NIGHT! THIS FACE PACK IS SUPPOSED TO WORK WONDERS.

SHAME! BUT NEVER MIND, CINDY. WE'LL EXPLAIN TO ALL THE DISHY FELLAS THAT YOU COULDN'T MAKE IT.

YEAH, AND WE'LL DANCE WITH THEM ALL, TOO. JUST FOR YOU!

IT'D HAVE TO! IT'S NOT FAIR. THEY'RE DELIBERATELY TALKING ABOUT THE DISCO TO ANNOY ME. AND, WHAT'S WORSE—IT'S WORKING!

And Thursday evening was even worse . . .

I'M GOING FIRST! YOU'LL USE ALL THE HOT WATER.

BUT YOU TAKE HOURS! I'LL MISS THE DISCO IF I HAVE TO WAIT TILL YOU'RE READY!

THAT'S YOUR HEM FINISHED NOW, IVY.

THANKS, CINDY. IT'S GREAT HAVING YOU AROUND. YOU'RE SO . . . SO . . .

So Cindy was left on her own —well, almost . . .

THAT'S EXACTLY WHAT SHE IS—SO- SO! COME ON OR WE'LL BE LATE. AND WE DON'T WANT TO MISS ALL THE DISHIEST FELLAS.

'BYE THEN, CINDERS DEAR. HAVE A NICE TIME!

MUCH AS I LOVE YOU, BROTHER CHRISTOPHER, I'D RATHER BE AT THE DISCO TONIGHT WITH A BOY A LITTLE BIT BIGGER.

She grew more and more miserable . . .

THIS IS AWFUL, I CAN'T READ ANY MORE OF CINDERELLA OR I'LL BURST INTO TEARS! I WISH I KNEW WHERE TO GET MY HANDS ON A FAIRY GODMOTHER LIKE HERS . . .

Wouldn't a fairy goodneighbour do just as well?

MRS PATERSON! WHAT ARE YOU DOING HERE?

MY HUSBAND HAS HAD TO WORK LATE TONIGHT. WE'RE NOT GOING OUT TILL ABOUT NINE SO I CAN BABYSIT FOR A LITTLE WHILE AFTER ALL.

SO YOU SHALL GO TO THE BALL OF FIRE, CINDY. THAT IS, IF YOU STILL WANT TO . . .

IF? OH, MRS PATERSON, YOU'RE WONDERFUL!

And before you could say . . . abracadabra . . .

JUST REMEMBER TO BE BACK FOR NINE, DEAR. MY BERT WILL WANT—

DON'T WORRY, I'LL BE HOME ON TIME.

She took a taxi to save time.

THIS'LL PROBABLY COST A BOMB, BUT WHO CARES? AT LEAST IT'LL GET ME THERE BEFORE ALL THE UNATTACHED GUYS ARE SNAPPED UP.

And guess who was trying to do the snapping?

HANDS OFF! HE'S ALREADY DANCED WITH YOU SIX TIMES! HIS FEET MUST BE BLACK AND BLUE BY NOW!

GET LOST! HE'D RATHER DANCE WITH ME THAN HAVE YOU SLOBBERING ALL OVER HIM!

TELL HER WE WANT TO BE ALONE, HANDSOME. YOU CHOOSE WHO YOU WANT TO DANCE WITH.

OK, I'LL CHOOSE.

And . . .

EXCUSE ME, I JUST SAW YOU COME IN. WOULD YOU LIKE TO DANCE?

YES, I'D LOVE TO. THANKS!

IT'S ME WHO SHOULD BE THANKING YOU. YOU JUST SAVED ME FROM A FATE WORSE THAN DEATH! THOSE TWO ARE—

BEFORE YOU SAY ANY MORE I'D BETTER TELL YOU—HEATHER AND IVY ARE MY SISTERS.

AND WHATEVER YOU SAY ABOUT THEM—I'LL WHOLEHEARTEDLY AGREE WITH!

HEATHER AND IVY? WELL, MAYBE THEY'LL GROW ON ME, BUT I DOUBT IT!

HMPH! LITTLE VIXEN! SHE CERTAINLY GOT HER CLAWS INTO HIM FAST ENOUGH.

THE POOR GUY NEVER HAD A CHANCE!

MY NAME'S CHARLIE—CHARLIE PRINCE! AND I RECKON I'VE JUST FOUND MY PRINCESS FROM A GOLDEN PALACE.

SOME PALACE! I LIVE IN THE HIGH-RISE BLOCK AT SHOREDITCH!

That night Cindy had a magical time. But before she knew it . . .

OH, HELP! IT'S AFTER NINE O'CLOCK!

SO, WHAT'S WRONG WITH THAT?

I'VE GOT TO GO— I PROMISED I'D BE BACK BY NINE! I'M SORRY, BUT I'M LATE AS IT IS . . .

I'M SORRY, TOO. I DON'T HAVE A CAR. BUT . . . WAIT PLEASE!

WELL, HELLO THERE. ARE YOU LOOKING FOR LITTLE OLD ME?

FORGET HER, CHARLIE. COME WITH ME AND LET'S BOOGIE THE NIGHT AWAY . . .

Some time later, back home . . .

OH, MRS PATERSON, I'M SORRY I'M LATE. I RUSHED ALL THE WAY, THEN THE HEEL ON MY SHOE BROKE . . . THEN . . .

DON'T WORRY, DEAR, JUST AS LONG AS YOU HAD A NICE TIME. BUT I'D BETTER GET A MOVE ON NOW.

NICE? IT WAS BEAUTIFUL . . . BUT SAD, TOO. I DON'T KNOW CHARLIE'S ADDRESS OR PHONE NUMBER OR ANYTHING. I'LL PROBABLY NEVER SEE HIM AGAIN.

Cindy's sisters didn't make her feel any better when they finally got home . . .

OOH, WHAT A HEAVENLY NIGHT! EVERYONE SAID I DANCED AS IF MY FEET WEREN'T TOUCHING THE FLOOR.

AND THEY'VE ALL GOT THE BRUISES ON THEIR FEET TO PROVE IT! WHAT A SHAME YOU HAD TO LEAVE SO EARLY, CINDY. WE HAD THE GUYS SWARMING ROUND US AFTER YOU LEFT.

I- I DON'T CARE ABOUT ALL THE GUYS—JUST CHARLIE! BUT I RECKON IT'LL TAKE A REAL FAIRY GODMOTHER AND A MAGIC WAND TO GET US TOGETHER AGAIN.

Perhaps not, because early next morning . . .

WHAT ON EARTH'S THAT RACKET GOING ON OUTSIDE?

And . . .

HELLO, THIS IS CHARLIE PRINCE! WILL THE BEAUTIFUL GIRL I DANCED WITH AT THE DISCO LAST NIGHT PLEASE GIVE ME A WAVE OR COME DOWN? I'VE GOT TO SEE YOU AGAIN . . . WHOEVER YOU ARE!

HE—HE'S FOUND ME. HE'S ACTUALLY REMEMBERED WHERE I LIVE AND COME LOOKING FOR ME!

MYSTERY NAME CROSSWORD

Are you clued up on what's happening in the pop, film or TV world? Well, here's your chance to test your skill with this super-sized, bumper Mystery Name Crossword.

All you have to do is solve the crossword clues, then unscramble the letters in the marked squares to find the name of a famous personality.

You'll find the answers on page 60 — but no cheating, 'cos guessing's half the fun!

Clue to Mystery Name: This guy skated his way to success.

CLUES ACROSS.

1. This international beauty contest is shown on TV (4, 5).
6. Words set to music (5).
9. A TV time lord (2, 3).
10. Tina, Simon and Christopher compere this TV show (4, 5).
11. Pupils at school or college (8).
12. An assistant of 9 across (6).
14. Not wild (4).
16. A TIN ALE is turned into a girl! (Anag. 7).
18. One of your parents (3).
19. A supernatural event — often in the Bible (7).
21. The Old Whistle Test is this colour (4).
25. Horses need these people to compete in show-jumping events (6).
26. An Eastern European country or a Womble! (8).
29. You can eat this and it's part of a Hot pop group! (9).
30. I MOAN about this girl! (Anag. 5).
31. Musical sounds or paper money (5).
32. One of England's oldest universities (9).

CLUES DOWN.

1. Humble or unassuming (6).
2. Very fine wood dust (7).
3. Lennon and McCartney ----- most of the Beatles' hits (5).
4. Mechanical men (6).
5. Stewart Copeland plays this instrument (4).
6. A football fan is known as this (9).
7. This game is often played by girls (7).
8. Smith, Jones, Robinson, etc., are these (8).
13. Not the beginning (3).
15. Almond biscuits or cakes (9).
17. Debbie Harry and Suzi Quatro are this nationality (8).
18. It's "Alright Now" for pop-man Hegarty (3).
20. An old-time British soldier — or a holiday camp assistant! (3, 4).
22. Mike's a TV impressionist, with his own show (7).
23. Go with SUE, MUM to find the place where old objects are kept (Anag. 6).
24. What K9 is short for (6).
27. There's no hope for this person (5).
28. A sort of powder (4).

EXCUSES, EXCUSES!

ARE you a great one for making up excuses when the going gets tough? Sometimes the most original idea can get you off the hook, and on others it's too far-fetched. But you can get a lot of fun thinking them up! We spoke to a few people — famous and not so famous — and asked them to tell us about their best excuses . . . true or otherwise!

Allison Howe is a seventeen-year-old secretarial student from Huddersfield.

"It was my birthday last month and my boyfriend didn't give me anything. His excuse? He said there was nothing in this world good enough for me!

"He took me out for a meal, though."

Eighteen-year-old Barry Clark works in an insurance office in Sutton Coldfield.

"I've used so many excuses that I can't remember them all! A boy in my office has got a pretty good collection, though — things always seem to be happening to him.

"He didn't appear for work one day, and we all wondered what'd happened. Next day he came in and told us. He'd parked his car in the car park and had gone to get a parking ticket for it. He put the money in the machine — and the next thing he knew he woke up in hospital!

"Apparently, he'd got an electric shock from the ticket machine and he passed out! You should have seen the office manager's face when he heard the story!"

Phil Lynott.

On having scoffed a plateful of cakes. "The trouble is, you're too good a cook."

Sixteen-year-old Christopher Hamilton is a store assistant. He lives in Perth.

"I'm always making excuses — for things I've done, things I haven't done, things I *should* have done . . . ! I don't know how my girlfriend puts up with it all, but she does!

"I was late for a date once 'cos I fell asleep on the bus and ended up miles away. I told Susan, my girlfriend, and she wouldn't believe me! It was really funny — all those other times when I'd made up excuses and she'd believed them, and this time, when it was true, she didn't!"

Bob Geldof.

The snide excuse. "I didn't mean to insult you, but you have the kind of face that invites it."

Nineteen-year-old Derek Lee is at university in Durham, studying English.

"Last summer, I went for an interview for a job in London. I got all smartened up for it, wearing my one and only suit.

"On the train down, this stupid man spilt a whole glass of tomato juice all over me. I rushed to the toilet to sponge it off. I managed to get rid of most of it, but there was still this horrible sticky stain.

"I decided I couldn't go to the interview like that, so when I got to London I rushed into a shop to buy a new pair of trousers. I didn't have much time so I asked for a pair of size 34 Wranglers, paid for them and left. I didn't have time to try them on, I just hoped they'd fit.

I had to catch a connecting train out to Wimbledon — I was rushing about like a madman. On the train I nipped into the toilet to change my trousers. The tomato juice ones looked horrible, and I decided they were past their best anyway. I opened the window and flung them out. Then I opened the other parcel for the jeans — and there was a size 34 Wrangler shirt!

"It was awful! I ended up borrowing the guard's long overcoat to get out of the station. Then I had to go and buy *another* pair of trousers. I didn't even go to the interview — I was too shattered. And besides, I was late — and I don't think they'd have believed me when I told them why!"

Rita Ray, Darts.

On when it's the girl's turn to pay for the night out. "I was going to take us for a slap-up meal in a swish restaurant but then I knew you'd find it more fun having a hamburger in a shop doorway."

Caroline Mainwaring is fifteen. She's at school in Ipswich.

"I'm not a very good liar, so nobody ever believes any of my excuses. Some people're great at thinking up excuses, but I'm not!

"The other day I was late for school 'cos my rabbit died and I'd been quite upset. Everybody just laughed at me when I told them. It wasn't fair."

Thereze Bazar, Dollar.

On the excuse that went wrong. "I'm sorry I didn't recognise you but you've put on so much weight since I saw you last."

Sally Robertson's eighteen and a hairdresser. She lives in Wolverhampton.

"The best excuse I've ever heard was from a boy I used to go out with. He'd been two-timing me — I found out from one of my friends.

"He told me the reason he'd two-timed me was that I'd had a lot of school work to do and he didn't want to drag me away from it. So he went out with someone else instead!"

Seventeen-year-old Andy Smith is at school in Hounslow.

"I once lent one of my mates an LP I'd just bought — and he never returned it.

"I kept asking him for it back and he eventually said he wasn't giving it to me 'cos some of the songs were quite rude and he didn't think my mum would approve!"

Sting.

The excuse to end all excuses. "I know you followed me all evening to see who that girl with me was. But she was foreign and wanted to know how to get to the station. So I offered to show her but I was on my way to the pictures, then this restaurant, and had to pick up some things from my place.

"She just had to tag along until we reached the station."

Bonnie Tyler.

The great put-down to a girl who's been eyeing your clothes up and down.

"Sorry my dress is a bit crumpled, but it's just been flown from Paris especially for tonight, so what can you expect?"

Mandy Farmer's sixteen and is at school in Drumchapel.

"I'm hopeless at doing homework — and it's not that I can't do it, it's just that I always forget! One time, though, I had the perfect excuse — I couldn't read the teacher's writing!

"He'd written out the exercise we had to do and got it photocopied at the school office. When I got home I got everything organised to do my homework — and then I saw I couldn't read it! I could decipher some of the words, but not enough to make sense.

"When I told him next day he let me off with it!"

Tim Atack, Child.

For turning up at school. "Sorry I had to come to school today only I was feeling well."

Fiona Lewis is seventeen. She works for a haulage firm in Carlisle.

"I'm always late for work — so I've got a good stock of excuses! The time I needed an excuse most, though, was dreadful. I was on the bus going to work, and one of my contact lenses fell out when I sneezed.

"I panicked 'cos I'm as blind as a bat without my lenses — and besides, I knew my mum would kill me 'cos she'd paid for them! Anyway, I had everybody on the bus looking for this one silly little piece of plastic.

"Nobody could find it, and the conductor said that he'd help me with a good, thorough search when we got to the terminus and everybody got off. So there was I, the conductor and the driver, crawling along this bus, hunting under seats for a contact lens.

"We found it eventually — it was nestling in an empty crisp packet someone had thrown on the floor. Nobody believed it all, though, when I got to work — an hour and forty minutes late! And it was true!"

Eighteen-year-old Ronnie Cowling works in a garage in Bootle.

"The best excuse I ever heard was from a guy who came in to the garage to buy some petrol. He was a real, smarmy businessman, with a terrific car — a Mercedes, I think it was.

"Anyway, he came in and wanted his tank filled up. I did it, and then asked him for the money. He just looked at me and then drawled, 'My dear boy, I *never* carry cash.' He paid by cheque, doing it all with a flourish. He made me feel like a real village hick!"

Ray Sawyer, Dr Hook.

On doing the romantic bit on the cheap. "Sorry the flowers are all the same but people aren't very imaginative with their front gardens in our street."

the BJ
guide to good manners

Are you the kind of girl who opens her mouth and puts both feet right in it? Well, here's what you need . . .

THIS guide shows you how to avoid ghastly pitfalls in life which might trip you up. Follow our advice on what not to do, and you're sure to end up doing the right thing.

Meeting new people can cause problems, but you'll never go wrong if you remember . . .

"Where d'you work, and how much do you earn?" More important, never say nothing — unless you *don't* want to talk to them.

See, once you get the hang of it, it's easy, isn't it? Now you've met lots of nice new people, maybe there'll be a nice new boy among them who wants to take you out to

Never say, "Hello, can you lend me 50p till Friday?"; "Where on earth did you get that silly badge?"; "Oh no, it wasn't *you* I wanted to meet. Where's your good-looking brother?"; "You're fatter than you look in the photo!";

dinner. So how will you cope with that ritzy restaurant . . .?

Never seize the menu and cry, "What's the most expensive thing here, then?"; "Don't think much of this place!"; "Yeugh!! What's this stuff?" or "Look at that

weird woman over there. What on earth's *that* she's wearing?" You never know, it could be his favourite sister.

And even if you've fallen in love with this nice new boy, don't shriek, "Arthur, you are overwhelmingly sexy and I adore you!!" while he's trying to eat the pudding, either. That'll only embarrass him like mad.

Of course, not everyone you meet'll want to take you to the Ritz for caviare butties. In fact, some people are quite ordinary, but that doesn't mean they're not worth bothering about.

If you want to show what a lovely person you are, why not try opening a few doors for little old ladies with shopping bags! And remember to smile and say, "Thanks!" when people open doors for you! Yes, you too can be a little ray of sunshine!

But some other people aren't just ordinary. They are awful and say terribly rude things to you!

For some reason, some older people seem to think they've got the right to be horribly rude to you. If *you* say, "What a revolting hat you're wearing, Auntie Ivy," that is rude. If *she* says, "What a revolting dress you're wearing!" that is a sensible comment, made for your own good.

We've gone into a great deal of complicated research about this one, but we haven't come up with any answers. Just remember, it's harder to be polite to some people than it is to others.

So remember . . . never bite Auntie Ivy or say, "When you were young? When was that, then, 1843?"; "Don't criticise what I'm wearing, you always look awful," or "Look, you don't think I'm bothered what *you* think, do you?"

Go off and kick the furniture instead.

Most of the people you'll meet are pretty much like

you. Yes, that's right, most people are given to putting their foot in it. But they're really quite kind and they don't intend to hurt people's feelings.

So when one of them comes up with a great big tactless remark, *never* leap on them with cries of rage. Or when one of them tells you a painful secret, *never* rush off broadcasting it about the place. If one of them has done something she'd rather forget *never* point it out loudly to everyone else. Think about it — in ten minutes' time you'll probably be in the same situation and then what would you do?

OK, you might cry, now I know what *not* to do when I'm eating at the Ritz or having a job interview . . . but what *do* I do?? Where's this simple guide you promised us?

Well, as a matter of fact, there *is* a very short, easy guide to good manners. Think how you'd feel if someone else did or said what you're just about to say or do. If you'd hate it — don't do it! And if you've mistakenly forgotten your memory, try this splendid one-word pick-me-up — say sorry!

Try this, and you won't just be super-polite — you'll be a real BJ Supergirl!

Remember, you can always lie down and kick and scream for half an hour in the quiet of your own room when the strain gets too much for you.

But keep trying!

solution to crossword

Across — 1 Miss World, 6 Songs, 9 Dr Who, 10 Blue Peter, 11 Students, 12 Romana, 14 Tame, 16 Natalie, 18 Dad, 19 Miracle, 21 Grey, 25 Riders, 26 Bulgaria, 29 Chocolate, 30 Naomi, 31 Notes, 32 Cambridge.

Down — 1 Modest, 2 Sawdust, 3 Wrote 4 Robots, 5 Drum, 6 Supporter, 7 Netball, 8 Surnames, 13 End, 15 Macaroons, 17 American, 18 Den, 20 Red Coat, 22 Yarwood, 23 Museum, 24 Canine, 27 Goner, 28 Talc.

Answer to Mystery Name — ROBIN COUSINS.

answers to names in the frames

LEAVE IT TO FATE!

Meanwhile, down below, Fay was deep in thought . . .

I WONDER WHAT'S GOING ON IN THE ROOMS WITH LIGHTED WINDOWS? WHO ARE THEY AND WHAT ARE THEY DOING—THOSE SHADOWY FIGURES BEHIND CLOSED CURTAINS?

Y'KNOW, SOMETIMES I GET A BIT BORED LIVING UP HERE. DON'T YOU THINK IT'D BE KIND OF NICE TO BE MERE MORTALS FOR A CHANGE? LIKE THAT GIRL DOWN THERE . . .

NO, I DON'T! LOOK HOW UNHAPPY THEY ARE—ALWAYS ARGUING AND MAKING EACH OTHER MISERABLE!

YEAH, AND THAT GIRL AND HER BOYFRIEND WERE PRETTY GOOD AT IT, TOO! I SUPPOSE WE'LL HAVE TO SEE IF WE CAN HELP HER . . . HERE—HAVE A CUP OF AMBROSIA WHILE WE DECIDE WHAT TO DO.

I BET NONE OF THEM ARE AS LONELY AS I AM RIGHT NOW . . . LONELY AS IT'S ONLY POSSIBLE TO BE WHEN YOU'VE JUST LOST THE ONE YOU LOVE MOST.

She was wrong, though, because in one of the houses . . .

OH, HAZEL—I MISS YOU SO MUCH! WHY DID YOU HAVE TO GO OFF WITH THAT OTHER GUY? HE COULD NEVER LOVE YOU AS MUCH AS I DID . . .

M'M . . . LOOKS LIKE WE'LL HAVE TO DO SOMETHING ABOUT THESE TWO. CAN'T LET THEM GO ON BEING SO MISERABLE.

WELL, THAT'S WHAT WE'RE HERE FOR, ISN'T IT?

WHO ARE WE? WE'RE THE FATES, OF COURSE—THREE SISTERS . . . GODDESSES, ACTUALLY . . . WHOSE JOB IT IS TO RULE OVER HUMAN DESTINY!

AND THAT'S NOT AN EASY THING TO DO, I CAN TELL YOU. BUT WE DO OUR BEST . . .

I TOLD YOU I DIDN'T CARE . . . THAT I'D FOUND SOMEONE ELSE, DIDN'T I, HAZEL? IF ONLY IT WERE TRUE . . . BUT IT SEEMS THE WHOLE WORLD'S GOT A PARTNER EXCEPT ME!

LOOK AT THAT GIRL THERE—I BET SHE'S HURRYING TO MEET HER BOYFRIEND. WHAT WOULD SHE KNOW ABOUT AN ACHING HEART AND A MISERABLE FEELING OF EMPTINESS INSIDE?

OH WELL, I SUPPOSE I MIGHT AS WELL TAKE A STROLL. BETTER THAN SITTING HERE BROODING . . .

Further down the road, Fay had posted her letters and was making her way home . . .

HELLO, CAT! I BET EVEN YOU'VE GOT A BOYFRIEND SOMEWHERE—YOU LUCKY LUMP!

NO, YOU'RE WRONG—THEY DIDN'T MEET STRAIGHT AWAY, THESE TWO LONELY PEOPLE. LIFE HARDLY EVER WORKS OUT AS NEATLY AS THAT.

YOU SEE, SOMETIMES YOU'VE GOT TO SUFFER AND BE UNHAPPY IN ORDER TO ENJOY THE GOOD THINGS LATER.

THAT'S RIGHT. YOU WOULDN'T APPRECIATE THEM, OTHERWISE!

AND THAT'S WHAT MAKES OUR JOB SO DIFFICULT— GETTING A NICE EVEN BALANCE.

EVERYONE MUST HAVE THEIR SHARE OF HAPPINESS . . . BUT WE HAVE TO THROW IN A FEW BAD TIMES AS WELL.

OF COURSE, WE MAKE MISTAKES SOMETIMES. YOU KNOW THOSE AWFUL DAYS WHEN NOTHING GOES RIGHT? WELL, THAT'S WHEN WE'VE OVERDONE THINGS A BIT. WE'D PROBABLY BEEN OUT LATE THE NIGHT BEFORE!

NOW, GIRLS, WE'D BETTER STOP GOSSIPING. WE'VE GOT WORK TO DO, REMEMBER? LET'S SEE WHAT'S HAPPENING TO FAY . . .

I'VE POSTED THE LETTERS, MUM. THINK I'LL GET READY FOR BED NOW.

YOU KNOW, DEAR, YOUR DAD AND I ARE A BIT WORRIED ABOUT YOU. IT'S NOT GOOD FOR YOU, SHUTTING YOURSELF AWAY UPSTAIRS ALL THE TIME. WHY DON'T YOU GO OUT WITH YOUR FRIENDS SOMETIMES—OR WATCH THE TELLY WITH US? YOU'VE SCARCELY BEEN OUT SINCE . . .

SINCE PAUL WENT TO AUSTRALIA? NO, I JUST DON'T WANT TO, MUM. I . . . I JUST WANT TO BE ALONE.

BUT IT'S NEARLY TWO MONTHS! YOU CAN'T SHUT YOURSELF AWAY FOR EVER, DEAR.

OH, LEAVE ME ALONE, WILL YOU? YOU JUST DON'T UNDERSTAND . . . NO ONE DOES!

OH, PAUL! I—I THOUGHT YOU REALLY LOVED ME. I THOUGHT YOU'D COME BACK IN SIX MONTHS, LIKE YOU PROMISED. WHY DID YOU HAVE TO GO AND MEET THAT GIRL OUT THERE AND . . . AND FALL FOR HER? WHY?

I WAS SO EXCITED TO GET THAT LETTER—AND THEN WHEN I READ IT I FELT LIKE MY WHOLE WORLD HAD JUST FALLEN APART . . .

I ALWAYS THOUGHT WE OVERDID THINGS A BIT THERE, YOU KNOW. THERE WAS NO NEED TO HAVE MADE HER THAT UNHAPPY!

WELL, WE'LL MAKE HER EXTRA HAPPY ONE DAY—TO MAKE UP!

62

Let's take another look at Jeff . . .

THE RIVER SEEMS COLD AND MURKY AND UNFRIENDLY NOW — COMPLETELY DIFFERENT TO THE WAY IT LOOKED WHEN I WAS LAST HERE WITH HAZEL. IT WAS SPARKLING UNDER A FULL MOON THEN, AND . . . AND WE WERE IN LOVE.

THEN YOU MET THAT OTHER GUY . . . THAT SMOOTHIE AT JOE'S PARTY, AND . . . WELL, THAT WAS THAT. YOU DIDN'T WANT TO KNOW ME ANY MORE. I WAS JUST IN THE WAY. OH WELL, I'D BETTER GO BACK TO MY DIGS NOW—THIS IS MAKING ME FEEL EVEN WORSE!

FOR PITY'S SAKE, LET'S DO SOMETHING! I CAN'T BEAR TO SEE TWO PEOPLE SO MISERABLE!

NOW, DEAR, PULL YOURSELF TOGETHER. REMEMBER YOU'RE A GODDESS—WE'RE SUPPOSED TO BE ABOVE FEELING EMOTION AND USELESS THINGS LIKE THAT.

Then, one Saturday morning, Fay went shopping for her mum, and . . .

OH, NO—WHAT A MESS! THAT BOX OF EGGS MUST'VE SPLIT OPEN!

ER . . . CAN I HELP? I HATE TO SEE A DAMSEL IN DISTRESS. MUST DATE BACK TO THE TIME WHEN I WAS A KNIGHT IN SHINING ARMOUR IN A FORMER LIFE, OR SOMETHING!

WELL, THANKS—BUT I DON'T KNOW HOW YOU CAN HELP! EVERYTHING'S ALL STICKY . . . MY MUM'LL KILL ME!

I KNOW HOW YOU FEEL—I'M A REAL BUTTERFINGERS MYSELF . . . ALWAYS DROPPING THINGS!

I'M JEFF, BY THE WAY. LOOK—WHY DON'T WE HAVE A CUP OF COFFEE IN THAT SNACK BAR OVER THERE? THEY MIGHT LEND US A WET CLOTH TO WIPE THESE TINS AND THINGS WITH.

GOOD IDEA! OK, LEAD THE WAY . . .

He touched her arm, and Fay felt something stir within her . . . something that hadn't been there since Paul went away.

HER EYES ARE SAD AND SHE SEEMS KIND OF UNHAPPY. IT CAN'T BE JUST THE EGGS BREAKING . . . SURELY?

HE SEEMS NICE—BUT KIND OF BROODING AND DEPRESSED IN SOME WAY. I WONDER WHY?

Finally, Jeff broke the silence . . .

WANT TO TELL ME ABOUT IT?

WH- WHAT D'YOU MEAN?

YOU'RE UNHAPPY, AREN'T YOU? I CAN TELL.

WELL, YES. AS IT HAPPENS YOU'RE RIGHT, I AM PRETTY MISERABLE.

SOMETIMES IT HELPS TO TALK TO A STRANGER, YOU KNOW. AND I'VE A GOOD SHOULDER FOR CRYING ON! WHY DON'T YOU TRY IT?

So she told him about Paul . . .

. . . AND THERE YOU HAVE IT. HE . . . HE'S DECIDED TO STAY OUT THERE AND WORK ON THE FARM WITH HIS UNCLE. WITH THAT GIRL.

I'M SORRY, FAY. I KNOW ALL TOO WELL HOW YOU FEEL BECAUSE I'M IN THE SAME BOAT.

THE END

64

Scent With Love

Blue Jeans Beauty

GONE are the days when you could recognise a girl by the perfume she wore — nowadays she'll probably have several to choose from. And that's great, 'cos not only is it lovely for other people if you smell super — it's lovely for you, too. After all, if you know you smell good, you feel good. And if you feel good, you look good!

It takes years to create a new fragrance. Most perfumes are made up of dozens — sometimes hundreds — of ingredients, and when a new formula is created it's Top Secret and guarded like Fort Knox! That's why perfumes tend to be expensive. But it's worth remembering that the more expensive they are, the longer they'll last. So a cheap one that you have to keep applying could turn out to be dearer in the long run!

LOVE NOTES

Perfumes are made up of "top notes," "middle notes" and "base notes." The top note's that first heady impression you get when the bottle's opened. It fades after a short while, leaving you with the middle note.

This is the "heart" of the perfume, giving it its character and richness, and a good one should last 4 to 6 hours.

Once that has faded you get the base note, and that's what makes the scent cling to your skin, and not just evaporate into the air. It can sometimes be unpleasant, though, so this is when to reapply your perfume.

We say "perfume," but in fact, toilet water and cologne are more popular. They're not as strong but they still contain the same fragrance — and they're cheaper!

With so many different perfumes in the shops it's hard to pick just one! It helps if you ask yourself what you want it for. Is it for a special occasion or for everyday wear? It's best to choose something light 'n' fresh for daytime and keep the heavier, sweeter scents for parties.

YOUR NOSE KNOWS

Whatever you do, don't buy the first bottle you fancy — and don't buy a perfume just 'cos you like the advert for it on telly! Don't spray six different scents up each arm, either, then try to choose. Your nose won't know what's hit it!

In fact, it's best to test cologne rather than perfume as perfume's sometimes so strong it makes your nose numb!

Choose just two colognes and spray one on each wrist. Sniff the top notes, then go away and do something else. Sniff again in about an hour when the top notes will have faded and you'll get the real scent.

If you're not keen on either, don't rush back to the counter to spray two more on — you only get a mixture of smells. Wait till another day when the first two have completely vanished.

Another mistake some people make is letting the assistant spray a perfume on to her arm for you to smell it. What smells good on her may smell awful on you, 'cos no two people react the same way to a fragrance. The reason is that the perfume blends with the various oils of your skin to make a completely original smell.

Lots of things can change the scent. F'r instance, a fair-skinned girl will get better results from a delicate perfume than a dark-skinned girl — 'cos darker skins produce more oil. A perfume will last longer on a girl with oily skin, but it also tends to turn a perfume "sweet." Some medicines and also smoking can affect your skin's reaction to a scent, too.

Even the climate makes a difference! The warmer it is, the quicker the top notes evaporate and the base notes come through — which is why perfume sometimes smells sweeter and heavier in the heat.

Perfume should be applied to your pulse points. The best places are your throat, wrists, cleavage, the nape of your neck, behind your knees and the insides of your elbows and ankles. Funnily enough, it's not a good idea to dab it behind your ears — as your skin oils are often different there.

GET ON THE SCENT

There're five main types of perfume . . .

Floral — these are flowery, refreshing and light, but can sometimes be rather sweet.

Green — fresh, crisp and woody, like pine and cedar. Good for daytime.

Citrus — sharp and tangy, with lemon, orange and bergamot oils.

Oriental — rich and strong, they're based on aromatic Eastern woods and grasses, with musk, civet and ambergris added. They can be very sultry so are best left for evenings.

Modern — bright, cheery and cool, with mainly synthetic oils used. They're designed to suit an uncomplicated, active life.

To give you an idea which scents fall into which categories, here're some examples. There're loads more, though (we don't have enough space to print them all!) — so have fun finding the right one(s) for you!

FLORAL
Quelques Fleurs by Houbigant
Tea Rose by Perfumer's Workshop
Jontue by Revlon
Heaven Scent by Helena Rubenstein
L'Aimant by Coty
Original Formula Lavender Flower by Boots

GREEN
Essence Rare by Houbigant
French Fern by Morny
Tweed by Lenthéric
Anais Anais by Cacharel
Futura Goya by Goya
Piquant by Goya

CITRUS
Just Call Me Maxi by Max Factor
Aqua Manda by Goya
Caribbean Lime by Boots
Gingham by Innoxa
Rive Gauche by Yves St Laurent
Cavale by Fabergé

ORIENTAL
Chantilly by Houbigant
Intimate by Revlon
L'Orientale by L'Oreal
Havoc by Mary Quant
Sandalwood by Morny
If by Lenthéric

MODERN
Charlie by Revlon
Smitty by Coty
Laughter by Yardley
Blasé by Max Factor
Fiori by Boots No. 7
Stevie B by Max Factor

So go on — be scentimental and buy yourself a little romance!

Footprints in the Sand

Sue Papworth

THE shore was always special to us. In the summer, early, before the visitors came down the cliff path to spread bright-coloured towels and deckchairs along the sea's edge, we ran together along the amber sands. And in the long, golden evenings we swam together in the still-warm sea and our hands met beneath the gently lapping waves, as our laughter echoed back at us from the cliffs.

When autumn came, and the gulls called in the colder, salty winds that swept in from the bay, we still came, our jacket collars turned up, and long scarves wound about our necks and blowing in the breeze.

In a sheltered place among the rocks, we kissed, and the sea murmured gently to us, kindly, as though it understood.

It was even our special place in the winter: the shingle crunched beneath our feet, and we watched as the grey waves came rolling in across the bay to break in thunder on the shore. In the crisp winter days, my hand was warm in yours. It was beautiful, then, and it belonged only to us, and the sea shared the secret of our love.

And then today we walked along the shore again together — a perfect, golden day, with the sun sparkling on blue water, and the sun high in a clear sky.

The sea whispered gently as we passed by, and I smiled up at you, remembering all the times we'd whispered our secrets to the sea.

But your eyes were far away, gazing out over the wide blue sea.

Behind us, our footprints stretched away the length of the shore, and ahead the sand was firm and clean and clear. I ran ahead of you, laughing, so happy at being with you.

Then I knelt to write in huge letters in the sand, *Derek* and *Jenny* and I enclosed our names in a heart that was bigger than both of us.

When you came up, you stood and watched me, but you didn't smile, and when I stood and took your hand, you looked away.

On the harbour wall you told me you were going away. Part of your life was over now — the part that I had shared. You said goodbye, and you went away, leaving me alone and desolate.

So I walked back alone, along the shore, hearing the sea murmuring gently and sadly to itself, and its salty tears of spray mingled with the tears on my cheeks, because the sea understands all about sadness and parting.

And when I reached the place where I'd linked our names in love, I saw that the sea had carried them away as if it all had never been, and the waves had wiped out our mingled footprints as though we had never walked there together in all the history of the world . . .

Goodbye Goodbyes!

Isla Dewar

WAKE and stare up at the ceiling. What's today? Tuesday, and Tuesday's Russian for beginners. Monday's yoga, Wednesday's tap dancing (blush, well, it's an old secret fantasy to tap dance). Thursdays I meet a few mates, for a chat.

Fridays we go, Daniel and I, to a dog-training class. Daniel the spaniel is not amused by this. He isn't at all enthusiastic about the idea of sitting and staying and walking to heel.

That leaves Saturdays and Sundays free for me to miss Andy and generally moan and sigh about missing Andy. Oh, how I long for Saturday and Sunday, all the activity is driving me crazy! It was Mum who first suggested it. I suppose she was right enough. To tell the truth, my behaviour was making her cross. "If you sigh just one more time," she would hiss between her teeth, "I'll . . . I'll . . ." She never did tell me what she'd do.

It all started when Andy went to college, and I went to pieces. I hadn't realised how much I relied on him. Well, he was round most nights and we went everywhere together. Then suddenly he was gone. Nothing. It left me wandering from room to room moping and mooching and feeling sorry for myself.

Mum said I'd better find something to take my mind off things. And that's when I started with the evening classes.

"Sue, are you up yet?" Mum calls now.

"Yes," I call from the depths of my downie, "be down in a sec."

"Only," adds Mum, "there's someone here to see you."

Big deal. It'll just be Mrs Harris from next door round for me to do her hair. Well, that's what I am really — a hairdresser. I don't mind, and the money's handy.

Money, now there's the reason for my ache. We are victims, Andy and me, of the money crisis. I mean, have you seen the price of rail fares recently? Wow! Time was when Andy and I could see one another every two or three weeks, but now we hardly meet at all during term time because the fares are too high. Three years he's been away now. Three years and galloping inflation has wrecked my love life!

"Sue!" It's my mum again. "Will you get up? There's someone here wanting to see you. Come downstairs this minute."

"I'm up!" I say, and cuddle down again. It's so cosy in here. Also I have this problem about getting up on Tuesdays. After all the deep breathing and slow stretching of last night's yoga, getting up is painful. 'Course, it hasn't always been yoga and Russian for beginners, there was floral art and still-life painting — I was quite good at that. Before Russian, I took conversational French, before that conversational Italian, German and Spanish. But I've forgotten most of it.

"Bonjour" — I remember that one, and "adieu." Goodbye, I'd have to remember that. It's the saddest thing about seeing him. You know it's only for a while and then it'll be goodbye again.

We're always saying goodbye, trying not to cry at the station. Goodbye and see you and sometimes he runs his fingers through my hair and whispers, "Love you." And I love him.

"Susan! Will you get UP?"

Oh, she's getting really mad now. She'll be up here in a minute and discover the truth. I'd better make the effort. Heave my weary body into the day. Wriggle and squeeze into my jeans. Checky shirt and that's me for the day. Run my fingers through my hair. It'll do.

The Last Farewell

Jo Reade

When goodbye seems to be the only word . . .

THERE'S something I've got to tell you, Mike. But I don't know how to begin . . .

It's a beautiful day. The sun's shining in a lovely blue sky and birds are singing. Reminds me of the day we first met.

No, that's not true. We first met at the disco, didn't we? You were with that Sandra Maxwell but you kept looking at me and I couldn't take my eyes off you. I thought you were gorgeous.

But I mean that other day when it was sunny and warm like this and the fair had come to the common. And I went with Marge and Sue and felt quite giddy and sick after a ride on the big dipper. So I thought I'd better go home. I didn't want to spoil their fun.

And then suddenly you were there. You asked me if I felt all right. I must have looked a bit pale. Then you said you'd walk home with me and I started feeling better straight away.

We took the short cut down the lane and stopped at that rickety old gate and just looked out over the fields, all green and speckled with flowers and sort of peaceful in the sunshine.

And then, do you remember, Mike? You told me you'd finished with Sandra, and when I asked why you said, "Because I saw you," and it was just like those love stories you read and don't believe. Because things like that don't happen, not in real life.

But they do.

I remember your words, "Because I saw you," and I knew what you meant. I felt the same. You'd been in my thoughts from that time in the disco. And we hadn't even spoken then, just looked at each other.

And I remember our first kiss. It was right there at the rickety gate, before I even knew your name or you knew mine.

That's why I don't know how to tell you why I'm here today, how to explain . . .

Don't take any notice of these tears. I'm not unhappy, not now. I'm fine, really I am. It's just that remembering all those good times with you always starts me off.

What I want to tell you is . . . I know you'll understand . . . there's someone else. Another boy. I thought it could never happen again, falling in love. I thought you were the one and only love I'd ever have.

When I first met Steve, I tried to resist whatever it was that attracted me to him. I was quite nasty to him. But he didn't give up and in the end I couldn't fight my feelings any more.

And I'm in love. That's what I want to tell you, Mike. I've found love. And it's magic and beautiful, the same as the love we had — but different, too. Not better — just different. I wish I could explain. I wish I had the words. But you do understand, don't you?

It's not that he's taken your place. No-one could do that. But now I know I can be happy again. My heart hasn't dried up the way I thought it had for so long, after . . .

It's silly, but I think that girl and that boy, you and me, are still standing by the rickety gate, looking into each other's eyes and seeing wonderful dreams for ever.

But there's no future, no other day when the boy says goodnight to the girl and kisses her and rides away on the shiny new motorbike he's so proud of and . . .

It's been over a year since that other day. When they told me what had happened I wanted to die, too. I thought that way I could still be with you. But I didn't die. For the living, life goes on.

I'll never forget you, Mike, you know that. And I'll still come and bring flowers and lay them here at your grave. Don't mind the tears, they're only memories. I've found another happiness and I know you would want me to be happy.

Goodbye, Mike, my lovely Mike . . .

I clatter downstairs. "OK, Mum, here I am." She's standing in the hall waving her hand at the kitchen. "In there," she says. "In there."

All very funny. Still, if that's where old Mrs Harris . . . only it isn't Mrs Harris, is it? It's Andy, smiling at me. And Mum looking all soppy.

"He wouldn't let me tell. It had to be a surprise."

And Andy pulls me on to his knee. "Hello, Sue. How're you?"

"Stiff," I say.

We kiss and kiss some more.

"So what are you doing here?" I ask.

"I'm home, home to stay. Took my finals, didn't I? And then I got a job back here while I wait for the results."

"Don't they mind?" I say. "I mean, don't you have to stay till the end?"

He shakes his head. We kiss again and I can feel his breath on my cheek and his arms round me. And now it's dawning on me that I've got a whole new set of goodbyes.

Goodbye to yoga and Russian for beginners, to tap dancing, though I'll miss that, to dog-training classes – wag your tail, Daniel! To pottery, to still-life painting, to conversational French.

And most of all, it's goodbye to saying goodbye.

I LOVE YOU BECAUSE...

I love your crazy grin, I love your dreamy eyes — but it's the silly little things you do that make me really care.

I love you . . .

because every time we go to the pictures you buy me a box of fruit gums — my favourites. And as if that isn't generous enough, you nearly always let me have the black ones. Such kindness, such consideration! I love these qualities in a bloke.

because you never, ever wear Crimplene trousers. Well, it's hard to get passionate about guys in Crimplene trousers. Or guys with silver medallions hanging neatly outside their shirts — which are usually left unbuttoned to the waist, showing off their manly chests. Yugh! Hairy chests, thick and heavy — like the coconut matting we used to leap about on at gym.

because you don't have a hairy chest!

because you don't try to beat me when we're watching "Mastermind." You never answer more questions than me and we're both equally dumb about Tudor England and European Ironing Boards 1886-1892.

because you've got influence. Your cousin Ernie's the conductor on the number 31 bus and you can get us on even though it's full. I just love being important like that.

because you do a really terrible imitation of David Bowie. It makes me giggle, and it's just as bad as my impersonations of Margaret Thatcher and Kate Bush.

because you don't mind sitting chatting to my dad about how he nearly got signed up for Millwall, while I'm taking far too long to get ready.

because you've got gorgeous eyes. 'Specially the bits at the corners that go all crinkly when you smile.

because you don't bore me with the intricasies of your brother's motorbike which you take apart on Saturday afternoons and put back together again. And I know you're just dying to natter on and on about it.

because you can dance. And I know we look good together at the disco.

because you remembered my birthday even though I thought you hadn't. You gave me a silver chain with a little heart on it, and I'll wear it forever and ever.

because you never let me down. You're always where you say you're going to be. And you've always got a special smile for me.

because you wear the aftershave I gave you last Christmas, and you smell great. All spicy 'n' nice.

because you don't mind me swooning and drooling over Sting. And I don't mind you getting tingles watching Debbie Harry — it's a good understanding we've got there.

because you always hold my hand wherever we go. I've sort of got used to that, so now my hand feels empty without your hand in it.

because you came round the other day and caught me in my curlers, and it didn't put you off. Thanks for that.

because I feel comfy with you. Well, it's like wearing my old pink fluffy slippers which are cosy and moulded to my feet. I'm used to them and I'm used to you. And I love you 'cos you don't mind my pink fluffy slippers which I know are really grotty.

because you kiss me so nicely. It's lovely and warm and I can feel your cheek next to my cheek — I like that. And when you hold me next to you, I feel your arms around me and it's got to be the nicest feeling in the world.

because you don't nibble my earlobes when Mum's just next door in the kitchen 'cos it makes me go all squirmy. Well, hardly ever, that is!

because after we've watched the late night horror film together you don't mind checking out the hall just to make sure there're no aliens from other planets there. Which is really brave of you 'cos if there were — you'd get eaten first.

because you love me. And I know — 'cos you're always telling me so!

Feeling Crafty?

IT'S IN THE BAG

Make this original, quilted bag in an evening and it'll see you through all the parties and discos of the season.

All you need is . . .
3 pieces of material
    42 x 27 cm
1 piece of Terylene wadding
    42 x 27 cm
6 metres silky cord
1 button or toggle
1 skein embroidery thread
plus sewing and tacking thread.

1. Sandwich the wadding between two of the pieces of material. (We used pink lining material as it has a nice sheen to it, and it's cheap, too!) Tack the three layers together round the outside edge and across the middle both horizontally and vertically (see sketch).

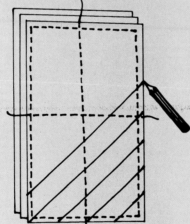

2. With a pencil, draw lines diagonally across the fabric 4 cm apart. Now sew the three layers together along these lines. This gives the rich, padded effect. You could leave it like this, but we sewed over the lines of stitching with purple embroidery thread to emphasise the pattern.

3. Take out the tacking stitches, and lay the third piece of material on the right side of the quilting, then sew together round the outside, 1½ cm from the edge, leaving a gap. Turn the right way out and sew up the gap.
Fold up the shorter end of the material 17 cm and sew up the sides, making the pocket of the bag.

4. Sew the cord right round the edge of the bag, twisting it into a loop when you come to the middle of the front flap. You'll have masses of cord left over, but don't worry — you'll need it to get the thickness of the shoulder strap.
Double the whole length and knot the ends together. Next, loop it round a door handle and, keeping it taut, twist the two pieces together. When you've twisted it all, carefully slip it off the handle and again place the two ends together. You'll find that this time they twist together of their own accord and all you have to do is smooth them evenly to get the lovely thick twisted strap in the picture.

5. Sew the ends firmly to the inside of the top corners of the pocket, and add a button or toggle to the front where the cord loop can catch round it to hold your bag shut.
And there you have it — a super, original handbag which is big enough to carry all you need at a disco, and light and pretty enough to sling round your shoulder while you dance.
Have fun!

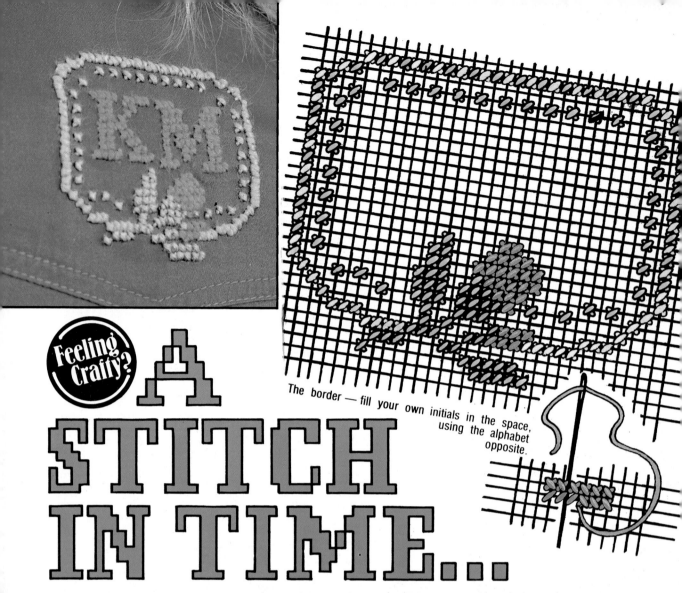

Feeling Crafty?

A STITCH IN TIME...

The border — fill your own initials in the space, using the alphabet opposite.

... saves your clothes from a whole lot of boredom!

CROSS-STITCH embroidery is so simple and yet it can transform the plainest of fabric into something really eye-catching. To get you started, we've chosen a rose-decorated border, into which you can put your initials, and add your own personal touch to jackets (as we've done here), jeans, shorts, tops . . . anywhere. Here's how . . .

Gather together . . . a scrap of embroidery canvas — 12 cm square will be plenty — plus a few skeins of Tapisserie wool or embroidery cotton or oddments of fine knitting wool, and a needle with a large eye.

Using a long, tacking stitch, attach the canvas to the spot where you want the embroidery to be. Then, using our diagrams as a guide, and counting each square of the chart as a square on the canvas, start filling in the pattern.

You can make each cross separately, or make a whole row of half crosses then go back to finish them off. Always make sure the top stroke of each cross goes in the same direction or the finished result will be messy.

Be sure to sew right through to the back of the material, too. The canvas is only a guide and will be pulled out when you've finished, so if you only embroider on the surface of the canvas your stitches will disappear later!

For the same reason, stitch right in the centre of each square, being careful not to catch any of the threads of canvas. If you do you'll find it too difficult to get rid of the canvas when you've finished.

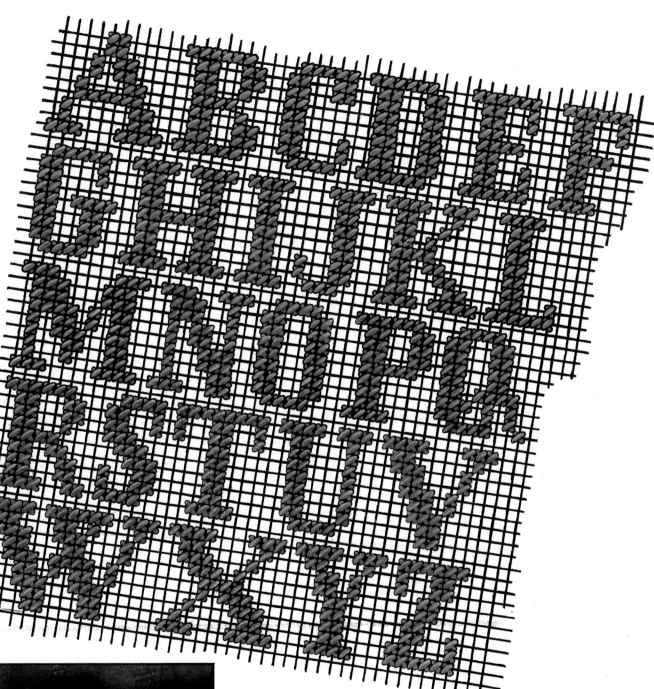

1. Here's the blank canvas tacked in place . . .

2. . . . and the finished embroidery on the back of the jacket.

3. And here you can see how the canvas is pulled away, strand by strand. You need patience for this, but it's worth it.

If you'd like to do more designs now, here's a super book to look out for. Cross-Stitch Embroidery by Kerstin Lokrantz, is published by Penguin, costing £2.50.

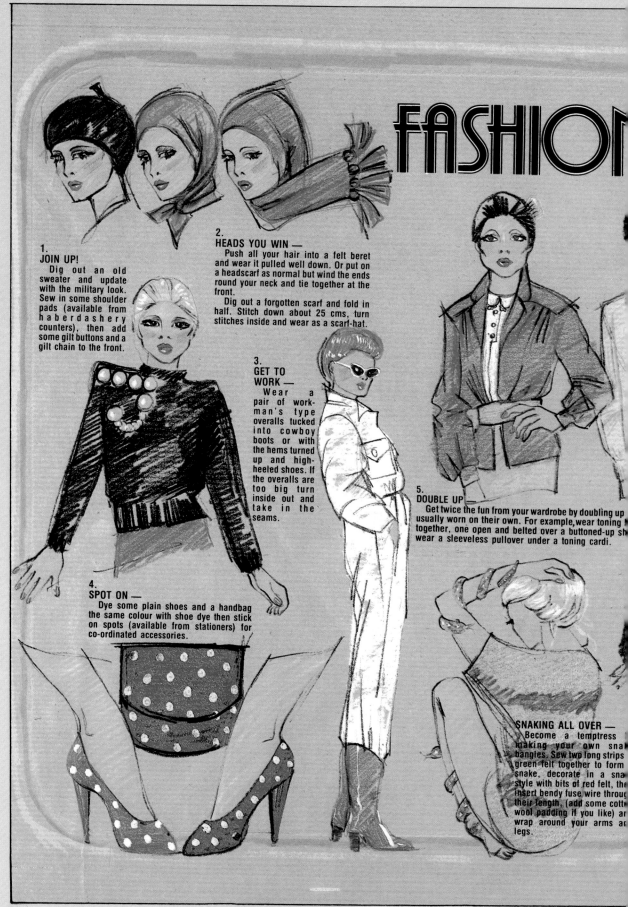

FASHION

1.
JOIN UP!
Dig out an old sweater and update with the military look. Sew in some shoulder pads (available from haberdashery counters), then add some gilt buttons and a gilt chain to the front.

2.
HEADS YOU WIN —
Push all your hair into a felt beret and wear it pulled well down. Or put on a headscarf as normal but wind the ends round your neck and tie together at the front.
Dig out a forgotten scarf and fold in half. Stitch down about 25 cms, turn stitches inside and wear as a scarf-hat.

3.
GET TO WORK —
Wear a pair of workman's type overalls tucked into cowboy boots or with the hems turned up and high-heeled shoes. If the overalls are too big turn inside out and take in the seams.

4.
SPOT ON —
Dye some plain shoes and a handbag the same colour with shoe dye then stick on spots (available from stationers) for co-ordinated accessories.

5.
DOUBLE UP
Get twice the fun from your wardrobe by doubling up usually worn on their own. For example, wear toning together, one open and belted over a buttoned-up sh wear a sleeveless pullover under a toning cardi.

SNAKING ALL OVER —
Become a temptress making your own snak bangles. Sew two long strips green felt together to form snake, decorate in a sna style with bits of red felt, th insert bendy fuse wire throug their length, (add some cotte wool padding if you like) ar wrap around your arms ar legs.

WORKSHOP

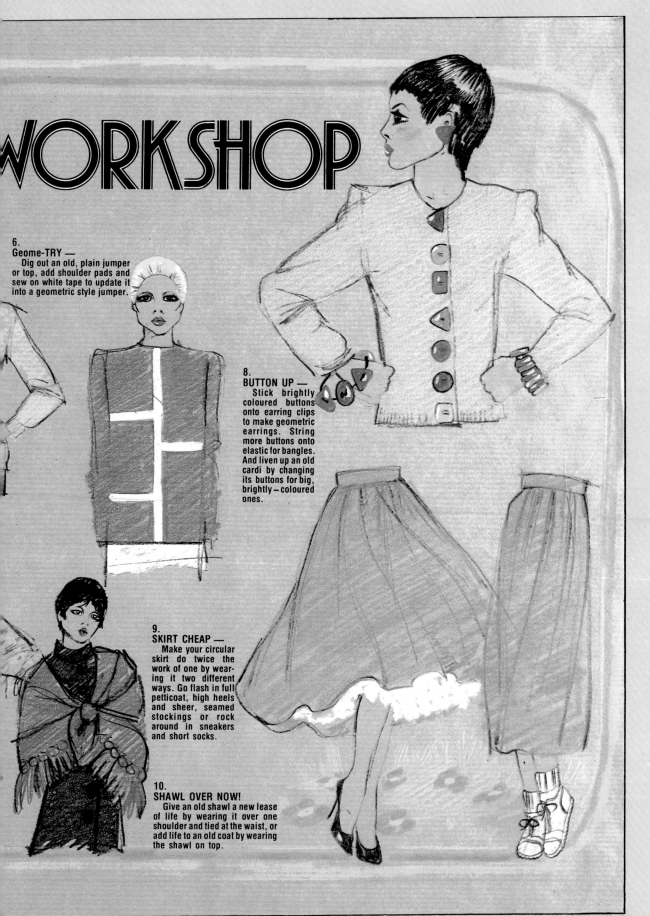

6.
Geome-TRY —
Dig out an old, plain jumper or top, add shoulder pads and sew on white tape to update it into a geometric style jumper.

8.
BUTTON UP —
Stick brightly coloured buttons onto earring clips to make geometric earrings. String more buttons onto elastic for bangles. And liven up an old cardi by changing its buttons for big, brightly—coloured ones.

9.
SKIRT CHEAP —
Make your circular skirt do twice the work of one by wearing it two different ways. Go flash in full petticoat, high heels and sheer, seamed stockings or rock around in sneakers and short socks.

10.
SHAWL OVER NOW!
Give an old shawl a new lease of life by wearing it over one shoulder and tied at the waist, or add life to an old coat by wearing the shawl on top.

WHEN YOU FALL IN LOVE...

it will be forever. That's how the old song goes, but real life isn't always as simple or straight forward . . .

WOULDN'T it be great if you could just skip first dates and jump on to the bit where you both decide you really quite like each other? But, unfortunately, everyone's got to put up with first dates — otherwise there might not be any seconds!

The worst thing about first dates is that you probably both feel a bit nervous of each other. That's only natural, 'cos you really don't know the other person all that well yet, do you? But this nervousness doesn't help much, either — all the shuffling about and long awkward silences could turn the night into an absolute disaster.

What you've both got to remember is — (a) he must have liked you enough to ask you out in the first place. (b) you must have quite fancied him too if you agreed to go out with him. If you remember this, it'll help turn the evening into a resounding success, instead of a dismal flop.

Here're some hints to help you along.

DON'T be late! First dates can be bad enough without leaving the poor guy hanging around, waiting for you to put in an appearance!

DO make a bit of an effort to look clean, tidy and presentable. OK, it may sound boring — but would *you* want to go out with someone whose jeans were held together with safety pins, and who obviously hasn't washed their hair since a week past Friday? No, 'course you wouldn't — and neither will he!

DON'T blabber on nervously, telling him about your Auntie Mabel's operation, and what your little brother did with his semolina pudding at tea-time. You don't have to go overboard trying to impress him!

DO make sure the conversation's a two-way thing. Ask him about his interests, what pop groups he likes, and so on. And if he asks you a question, try not to give just "Yes " or "No" answers. He could think you're bored to tears.

DON'T shuffle about from one foot to the other, saying, "Oh, anywhere really. I don't mind," when he asks you where you want to go. It doesn't look as if you're very *interested*, does it?

DO come up with a few suggestions of your own. Check what's on at the pictures before you go out, or find out if there're any good discos on. Of course, the best first dates are when you've decided beforehand where you're going to go!

DON'T get into one of those, "No, no, it's OK, I'll pay my own," "No, you won't — I'll pay, I asked you out" arguments.

DO let him pay if he insists. Most guys like to pay on your first night together — and if you're lucky there'll be loads of other nights you can offer to go halves, or even take *him* out!

JUST ME AND YOU

One of the best bits about going out with a guy you haven't known for very long, is finding out all the little things about him. Like how many sugars he takes in his tea, or what football team he supports!

But it's easy, after you've been out with him a few times, to take your fella for granted. You might turn up a bit late for dates — knowing that he'll wait for you. Maybe he will — it's just not very polite to keep him waiting, that's all!

And even though he came round one night, and caught you with your electric rollers in, that's no excuse for not taking care of your appearance. You don't have time to spend three hours getting ready for every date, of course, but do remember the basics — like brushing your teeth, and making sure you haven't got big rips in your tights.

Don't get too possessive too early. If you've only been going out with a guy for a month you've no right to start screaming when he wants to go out with his mates on Friday night, and you wanted to take him along to the disco so you could show him off to your friends!

You don't own him — so don't act as if you do!

AWAY FROM EACH OTHER

No matter how close you are to your guy, you both need some time away from each other. If you saw each other all day, every day, you'd soon run out of things to talk about!

So if he's absolutely mad about football, and you're not, don't force yourself to go along every Saturday to watch his team play.

Instead, now's a great chance for getting together with your mates. And let's face it, you'll get more fun out of going round the shops with your pals, than you would if it was just you and your guy.

Most guys can't understand the fascination of going into lots of different shops, trying on clothes, and testing out make-up. He'd only tag along behind you, moaning about how silly it is to try on twelve different jumpers if you're not going to buy anything!

And sometimes your guy won't want *you* around! If he's planning to take his precious Yamaha to bits (about five hundred and twelve bits, it seems to you!) then the last thing he'll want is you standing around moaning, "It's freezing, will you be long? *Top Of The Pops* is on in ten minutes." If you're an expert on motorbikes then he'll be glad to have you around, but if not you'll only get in his way.

HAVING FUN

Make sure you and your fella don't get into a rut! Going to the same places, week after week, doing the same things all the time can lead to loads of nasty arguments.

It's easy to get into the habit of going to the disco every Saturday night, the pictures one night during the week, and staying in the house a couple of nights. Not very exciting, is it?

Make sure you mix with other people. Foursomes can be fun, and going out in a big crowd can be fantastic. You get to hear everyone else's news, find out who's going out with who — and you've still got your favourite guy to walk you home!

Try going somewhere different on your nights out together. You could both take up judo at evening

classes, play tennis, go for a swim at the local pool.

Doing things is what's important. Sometimes it's nice just to sit down and talk things over, but if that's all you ever do, now's the time to change. You could end up thinking it's *him* who's boring when it's really the dates that're causing the problem!

DON'T ARGUE!

Arguments can be healthy sometimes! A good screaming match can sometimes help clear the air — and making up's the best bit!

Make sure you're not arguing *too* much, though, otherwise there could be one argument too many, and you'll both end up saying things you'll probably regret later.

A lot of arguments are caused by jealousy. Some guys don't like it if they hear a girl saying another guy's fanciable. And just think of the number of girls who burst into tears if they see their fella even *looking* at another female!

But real jealousy's the worst. It's horrible; it can make you imagine looks that weren't there, make you think you saw smiles you weren't meant to see . . . Some girls can get positively neurotic about it, and hurl accusations at some perfectly innocent guy.

So if you see your fella disappearing down the High Street with a beautiful blonde at his side — for goodness' sake ask him about it. If you don't, you'll probably just worry yourself sick and blurt out what you saw three months later. If you ask him next time you see him you'll save yourself a lot of heartache.

Either he'll say, "Oh, yes, that was my cousin. She was just helping me choose your birthday present," or, "Oh, I've been meaning to tell you. I'm . . . em . . . going out with her." At least you'll know one way or the other — without creating a fuss.

LET'S BE SERIOUS

You don't have to have a ring on your finger to be serious about your boyfriend! At the same time, there's no time limit set on it — so don't start listening for wedding bells just 'cos you've been together for a whole twelve weeks — or even twelve months!

Different relationships suit different people. Some couples are fairly casual about the whole thing. They enjoy being together, they've been going steady for a while, but neither of them have ever thought of settling down.

And why should they? They're perfectly happy as they are, so why spoil it by thinking of the future? Maybe they will end up getting engaged, or married, but for the moment they're perfectly happy.

Too many girls try to rush their boyfriends into getting engaged. To them, a ring is just a symbol, something to show off to their friends.

The thought of getting engaged or married is sometimes the last thing on a guy's mind — and it can be a bit of a shock if you suddenly drag him down to the jeweller's one Saturday morning and say, "Look, that's the kind of ring I'd like!"

An engagement is a promise to marry and it means you're both thinking of a future together. It's not something you should take lightly — after all, you've got to be sure you *want* to spend the next fifty years with this guy. It's nice to know he loves you, and wants to spend the rest of his life with you — but the worst reason in the world for getting engaged is because you don't want to hurt his feelings by saying "no."

So don't let yourself be rushed into anything you're not sure of. If he loves you enough he won't mind waiting till you're a hundred per cent certain you're ready for such a big step.

So there you are — you've got the beginning and the end — it's up to you to make the most of the bit in between!

BORN BEAUTIFUL

Our special zodiac beauty guide'll tell you what your best (and worst!) points are, according to when you were born. So now you can make yourself a star!

SMOOTHIE SKIN

That's the first thing people notice about **MISS AQUARIUS (Jan. 20-Feb. 18).** So if you're a lucky Aquarian with a peaches and cream complexion, our advice is to make sure it stays that way with a regular cleansing, toning and moisturising routine. You don't have to use anything expensive, with all sorts of added extras. The important thing is to do it every night — no falling asleep with your make-up still on!

Although your skin's usually clear and flawless, it can be a bit pale, so don't be afraid to brush a warm, tawny blusher over your cheekbones and very lightly around your hairline, tip of nose and point of chin. It'll really brighten up your face.

Exercise isn't a word you like to hear, but a spot of skipping (that's not too awful, is it?) will do wonders for your circulation and get your cheeks glowing!

FIGURE-PERFECT

MISS ARIES (March 21-April 20) has a super, curvy figure. You often eat like an elephant but you rarely have a shape like one! Keep things that way by making sure you get plenty exercise, and if you feel you're getting a little overweight start walking instead of taking buses.

It's the dreaded spots and pimples you've got to watch out for, so be sure to drink lots of water, eat plenty fresh fruit and vegetables, and go easy on greasy foods like chips and crisps.

Dry skin on the cheeks is often a problem for you so moisturiser is a must. Just keep it on the bits that need it, though — not all over your nose and chin!

disco even if you've been plodding round the shops all day!

TANTALISING TEETH

. . . make that **GEMINI** grin irresistible! A bright girl is our **MISS GEMINI (May 21-June 20),** 'cos she knows there's nothing puts the fellas (or anyone else, for that matter) off more than rotten teeth. So make sure you don't miss your regular dental visits. After all, even if you're terrified at the sound of the drill — you'd hate having false teeth even more!

Gemini folk also love to spend money on new things then rush home to try 'em out. You could have a lot of fun trying out different colour rinses on your hair, or unusual combinations of eyeshadow. With your sparkling looks you can get away with wearing all sorts of exciting new make-up.

Just don't forget to apply your lipstick extra-carefully to draw attention to those perfect pearlies — and blot it on a tissue so you don't get pink smears spoiling the brightness of your smile.

LUSCIOUS LIPS

. . . are usually what get **MISS PISCES (Feb. 19-March 20)** noticed — at least by all the fellas! So you owe it to yourself to make the most of that pretty mouth with lipstick and gloss, applied carefully with a proper lipbrush to get a smooth outline.

Pisceans often moan about lank, greasy hair. If that sounds like you, try washing it frequently (say every second or third day) but use the mildest of shampoos. Baby shampoo is just the thing. Wash once only and rinse in lukewarm water — not hot, as it stimulates the oil-producing glands to make your hair even greasier!

PRETTY FEET

They may not sound the most wonderful beauty asset, but **MISS TAURUS (April 21-May 20)** is clever enough to see that her tantalising tootsies keep her smiling and dancing the night away when everyone else's are blistered and tired.

You should wear comfy, lowish shoes during the day but invest in a pair of strappy, high-heeled shoes or sexy, open sandals to show off pretty feet to their best advantage. Painted toenails look great, too — 'specially if they match your outfit.

To get your toes tingling give yourself a mini pedicure by rubbing baby oil or hand cream well into your feet and ankles, then splashing with eau de cologne and dusting with a little talc.

On hot days mix the eau de cologne with icy-cold water and keep it in the fridge before you use it — it'll have you dashing to the

BIG, BEAUTIFUL EYES

These often belong to feminine **MISS CANCER (June 21-July 21)** — but, sadly, you don't always make the most of them. You tend to be a bit too unadventurous with eye make-up, either sticking to the same, safe shade, day in, day out, or not bothering with any at all!

You'd be well advised to stop spending so much on sweets and stodgy snacks (which aren't doing you any good, anyway) and spend it instead on an eyeshadow palette with loads of different shades in it. Then you can experiment till you discover how best to flatter those eyes.

Cancerians love pretty combs and slides for their hair, but if you're going to draw attention to it you should make sure you keep your locks clean and shiny.

You also love feminine scents so if you've got to meet a pal in town arrange for it to be at a perfume counter. Then you'll happily wait for ages.

THICK, SHINING HAIR

That's usually **MISS LEO'S** crowning glory, so if this is your star sign **(July 22-Aug. 21)** make the most of that glossy mane by getting it professionally cut and styled, then washing and conditioning it regularly. Herb shampoos full of natural products will keep your hair in tip-top shape, and so will a final rinse in pure rainwater. So remember to put out a bucket next time there's a shower!

You can often hear a Leo lady before you see her simply because she loves to jingle — with arms full of bangles and fingers full of rings — the more glittery the better! Next time you want to turn heads, why not carry the glitter-look right through — with gold shoes and belt and golden make-up? You'll really look wild!

HOLDABLE HANDS

. . . tipped with super-shiny nails can be found on **MISS VIRGO (Aug. 22-Sept. 21),** so a manicure set would be the perfect gift to help keep them in great shape. Virgo girls can condition their hands by rubbing in glycerine with a little lemon juice added.

You'll know it was worth the effort, too, when you're holding hands with your fella — he'll think their softness is so romantic and feminine!

You should resist the urge to shape your nails into pointed talons, though. They just won't look right on you. Use an emery board to file them into a gentle curve.

If you're a Virgo one problem you won't have is never being able to find your beauty kit. You ALWAYS put everything tidily away 'cos you hate not knowing exactly where everything is — and quite right, too.

MODEL-GIRL LOOKS

If you ever hear anyone say, "She's got such a pretty face!" we'd bet they're talking about **MISS LIBRA (Sept. 22-Oct. 22).** Libran girls are real charmers who love to flirt and turn on the allure when there're guys about. You rarely take a lot of trouble with your make-up (probably 'cos you don't really need any!), although you do enjoy wearing it.

Our advice is to make the very best of your super looks by taking that little bit more care over everything. Choose a flattering hairstyle to compliment your face shape.

Take special care of your eyebrows as they're often neglected. Pluck away stray hairs — from underneath and between brows only — to form a softly-curved arch. And don't forget to use a warm-toned blusher fluffed on to your cheekbones to bring your face "alive."

BAGS OF STYLE

. . . and enough sex appeal to make the fellas go boggle-eyed — that's what **MISS SCORPIO'S** got! **(Oct. 23-Nov. 21).** You may not be strikingly pretty . . . you may not have the world's most wonderful figure . . . but there's something about you — a sort of sparkle and liveliness — that attracts guys like bees round a honey-pot!

If you're a Scorpio femme fatale then see you get enough sleep because you need it more than most other star signs. Scorpios use up lots of energy, especially the nervous kind, and if you don't get your regular eight hours you begin to wilt.

Try not to wear too much make-up, either. We know you love to experiment and paint your face almost like an actress — but boys do tend to prefer a more natural look and you just might frighten them off!

LONG, LONG LEGS

If they're sleek, slim and seem to go on for ever, chances are they belong to **MISS SAGITTARIUS (Nov. 22-Dec. 20).** Always in a hurry, always broke, always hungry and nearly always happy — that's the typical Sagittarian girl.

You're full of energy and bounce — in fact, perhaps it's all the sports you enjoy that keep your legs in such great shape. You could really come into your own at the disco. Buy yourself a clinging body-suit or wear a tiny skirt with brightly-coloured tights and ultra-high heels. You'll look terrific!

To keep your legs looking their best, wear thick, warm tights in winter to stop your skin becoming red and dry — and in summer go bare-legged as much as possible to get a golden tan.

Exercise your feet, too, to keep your ankles slim. It's easy — just sit on a chair with your legs straight out in front of you and imagine you're stirring a bowl of thick custard with one foot at a time!

NOTHING WAISTED

. . . not around **MISS CAPRICORN's** middle, that is! **(Dec. 21-Jan. 19).** You usually have a super-slim waist, and neat hips, too — despite being a calm, capable type who rarely gets ruffled and likes nothing better than curling up in a chair with a good book. Lack of exercise never seems to give you a plump rump!

Show off your tiny waist by wearing a brightly-coloured, wild belt with your favourite dress. Soft suede or leather would look good on you — or try making your own belt, using satin over petersham. It's not only eye-catching, but inexpensive, too.

Allie had been crazy about guys who'd turned out to be rats before. But none of them had come between us the way Jeff had . . .

SHE BELIEVED HIS LIES!

I COULDN'T understand what was wrong with Allie when I walked into the classroom that morning. Something was. I'd realised that when she wasn't waiting for me as usual at the corner of the street.

And now, when I walked across to her, shouting, "Hi! What's up with you this morning?" she just turned her back on me and went on talking to Gill Fisher as if I didn't exist.

Then I heard her say, as I tried to get closer, and edge into the conversation, "Some people don't know when they're not wanted, do they?" in a really sneering voice.

I'd seen it happen to best friends before, one suddenly falling out with the other for no real reason at all. But I never thought it would happen to Allie and me. We'd always been close, right from when we were little.

In fact, only the night before, she'd been round at my house, crying her eyes out, and I'd listened to her, and tried to help her over it, the way she'd helped me, time and time again. I thought we'd sorted everything out between us. When she left she'd been smiling and laughing, just like her old self.

"Thanks," she'd said. "You're a pal!"

JUST ANOTHER LAYABOUT

Jeff was the problem. I'd never liked him, right from when we met him at the disco, but Allie had really fallen for him. She couldn't do anything by halves, especially if there was a boy involved. And some of the boys she'd liked! They were all more or less the same type — off-hand, unreliable and a bit wild.

Jeff was just another layabout, as far as I could see. But I couldn't tell Allie that, not when she was starry-eyed about him. I just had to sit back and say nothing and watch her being messed around by broken dates.

Until last night. He'd finished with her. That's what she'd come round to tell me.

SOME THINGS HURT FAR TOO MUCH

She was in a terrible state. Jeff had been the only thing she'd given any time or attention to for weeks, and now he'd finished with her, she was completely broken up.

It took me ages to calm her down. I had to tread really gently. I knew I couldn't tell her how relieved and happy I really was, I just had to try to make her realise that she was better off without him.

Some of the things I knew about Jeff Baines were better kept secret. Even to best friends, you don't tell everything you know. Some things hurt far too much.

I'd got the story out of her in the end. He'd met her from school on his motorbike, out of the blue, and she'd been over the moon thinking that for a change she'd be out with him on her own. Usually he took her along when he was with his mates, and sometimes he even forgot that she was with him. I didn't know why she'd put up with that sort of thing. I certainly wouldn't have done.

But he hadn't come to take her out. He'd just come to deliver a message that he'd decided he fancied someone else, and that he was packing her in.

I think the shock of it all hurt her more than anything. I knew she wasn't expecting it. She'd been telling me all along that Jeff was different from all the other boys she'd been out with — soft at heart, quiet, really, and quite romantic when he was in the mood.

She told me some of the things he'd said to her, little remarks she stored up to convince herself that this was the real thing.

She'd built her hopes on, "You're quite a girl for a kid of fifteen!" and, "I could really fall for you in a big way!" It wasn't a lot to go on. But Allie had thought he was the answer to her dreams.

I talked to her for ages last night. I pointed out all the times she'd been messed around by Jeff. I said we'd have a great time at the disco on Saturday, and that maybe she'd meet someone else.

I even told her that Gary Parker had been asking about her, even though that was a bit of an exaggeration. It was just that I knew she liked Gary Parker, and I wanted to start her off thinking about something or someone else.

And then, in the end, when she was starting to see sense, I told her just a few of the things I'd heard about Jeff — rumours, maybe, but close enough to what I knew about him to be probably true.

He never stayed with one girl for long, just long enough.

I told Allie she'd got off lightly, and she seemed to agree with me.

So why wasn't she speaking to me this morning? I thought we were back together again, looking forward to Allie's big night of freedom on Saturday when we were going to make a play for Gary Parker, and his friend, Mark, who I'd fancied for ages.

That's what we'd decided to do last night, planning and scheming the way we'd always done in the past, deciding what to wear, giggling over the best way to make it obvious to the boys that we liked them.

I had to find out what had changed her mind, and turned her against me.

"Hey, Allie! Why aren't you speaking?" I asked her. She didn't even turn round. She didn't take any notice of me. Then she said, in a loud voice to Gill Fisher:

"There's a terrible smell around here. I reckon it's coming from behind my back!" and Gill Fisher sniggered and said, "Push off, Debbie Coles. We're having a private conversation!"

I stood there, not knowing what to do next. There was a big lump filling my throat, but I was determined not to cry. I wasn't going to let Gill Fisher get under my skin. I didn't care about her. I just wanted Allie to explain.

"Just tell me why, Allie!" I begged, pulling at her sleeve. She shrugged me off, and then turned to me with a really angry look on her face. I'd never seen Allie look like that before, so full of hate — and I'd never expected her to look that way at me.

"Call yourself a friend?" she sneered. "Well, for your information, I'm back with Jeff, and you needn't look so surprised! I went round the café on my way home to tell him I was glad we were finishing, after what you'd told me about him!

"He put me right about you, Debbie Coles! He told me how you'd thrown yourself at him! You've been jealous of me all this time, haven't you? You wanted him yourself! Well, hard luck, 'cos he's mine, and you know what you can do with yourself!" And then she turned her back on me again, leaving me white and shaking.

TEARS

What could I say to that? There wasn't anything I could say. The tears I'd tried to hold back just trailed slowly down my cheeks. She wasn't in the mood to believe anything I could tell her now — and she wouldn't be, until she was free of that boy she'd gone back to.

The boy who'd asked me for a date, last night. The boy who'd threatened me when I turned him down. "You'll wish you hadn't!" The boy who'd come between me and my best friend.

He was even worse than they'd said he was, Jeff Baines. But Allie was going to have to find that out for herself now.

Even to best friends you don't tell everything you know. Some things hurt far too much.

WAIST WATCHERS
pull yourself together with a new belt

IT'S amazing how much a new belt can brighten up your appearance. You can wear one over jumpers, T-shirts, blouses, or even to hold up your trousers!

Belt an old shirt or even a coat or jacket and you instantly look smarter and slimmer. Even better if you make your own 'cos nobody else will have one quite like it!

Here're a few ideas to copy or adapt if you want a *very* individual look.

Comfy Cumberbund

Materials—1 large piece of felt (we used a remnant).

Small piece of felt in contrasting shade. Velcro or hooks and eyes to fasten.

To get the shape right make a paper pattern out of newspaper first.

Fold a piece of newspaper in half and from a fold outwards draw the outline of a triangle then draw a straight line to wrap round your waist. Open out the newspaper and you should have a shape similar to the one in the photo.

Cut out two of these shapes from felt, sew together leaving a gap for turning. Turn inside out to hide seams and press.

Secure at the back with Velcro or press fasteners and add a felt motif to the front in a contrasting colour.

Inch Clinch

Materials—Tape measure, sticky - backed plastic, buckle, eyelets (optional).

Cut the tape measure in half and line up halves so that you have a thick belt. Cover belt with sticky-backed plastic.

Attach buckle to belt with staples or strong glue. Make holes in the belt and leave them as they are, or strengthen with eyelets.

Soft Option

Materials—Felt, buckle.

Simply cut a large piece of felt into a wide belt, narrowing it down at the ends. Use pinking shears and you won't need to hem the felt.

Using small stitches, sew on a brightly-coloured buckle.

Two Tone

Materials—Length of Petersham, same length of narrow braid in contrasting colours, metal clasp.

Line up braid on top of Petersham and sew in place. Attach clasps to each end and stitch down as shown.

Hardy Hessian

Materials—Length of hessian tape, leather kilt buckle.

Cut hessian tape to fit your waist. Neaten ends by turning in to fit the width of the leather belt buckle. Using strong thread, sew on buckle.

Party Sparkler

Materials—1 metre of wide Petersham ribbon, metal belt clasp, two rolls of shiny, gift-wrap ribbon, glue.

Cut the Petersham to fit your waist plus a few extra inches so's you can attach the clasp. Lay Petersham out flat and carefully stick on similar lengths of contrasting gift ribbon.

Leave to dry then attach clasps by slipping end of belt around the bar of the buckle and keeping in place with a few stitches or staples.

In Stitches

Materials—1 ball of double knitting wool, 1 pair No. 8 needles, Velcro.

Cast on ten or more stitches, according to how wide you'd like your belt to be, and knit in stocking stitch until the knitted strip is long enough to fit your waist. Add a buttonhole a couple of inches from one end. Cast off.

Cast on 30 stitches and knit oblong for purse. Cast off when right size.

With right sides together, sew up sides of oblong to make a pouch. Turn right sides out and press.

Attach bits of Velcro tape to belt and purse and stick purse on to belt. Use another bit of Velcro to fasten the belt once you've threaded it through the buttonhole.

In The Pink

Materials—1 metre of broderie anglaise, flowery braid, Petersham, sticky - backed plastic, fastening, feathers or flowers.

Take enough broderie anglaise ribbon to fit round your waist. Thread through it a similar length of flowery braid. Sew this on to Petersham to give the belt a bit of body.

Finish off by covering the belt on both sides with see-through, sticky-backed plastic. Neatly fold under the ends and fasten the belt with Velcro, hooks and eyes or snap fasteners.

Cover the join with a bunch of brightly coloured feathers or flowers.

Braid to Measure

Materials—1 metre each of navy, white and red cord. Small packet of beads.

Tie the three bits of braid together at one end then plait them to about six inches from each end. Keep the plaits in place with a few stitches.

Unravel the braid at each end and thread a bead on each thread. Keep in place by knotting the thread at the end.

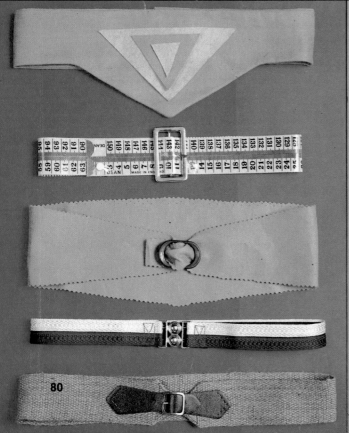

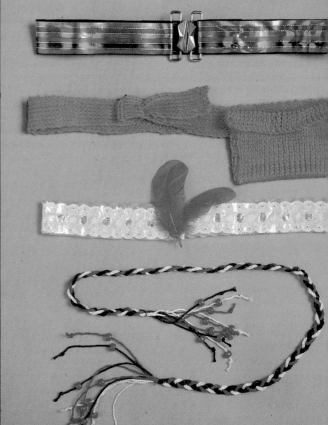

You Must Be JOKING!

These Gags Are Good For A Giggle!

Waiter, Waiter...

Waiter, waiter, there's a dead fly in my soup!
Yes, sir, it's the heat that kills them.

Waiter, waiter, what's this fly doing in my soup?
Looks like the backstroke, sir.

Waiter, waiter, there're two flies in my soup!
It's a special offer, sir.

Rotten Riddles

What's green and hairy and goes up and down?
A gooseberry in a lift.

How can you tell if there's an elephant in the fridge?
You can't close the door.

How do you milk a hedgehog?
Very carefully!

Why did the tomato turn red?
Because it saw the salad dressing.

What do you call a man who breaks into a meat factory?
A hamburglar.

How do you recognise an Irishman on an oil-rig?
He's the one throwing bread to the helicopters.

Where was the Magna Carta signed?
At the bottom.

Doctor, Doctor...

Doctor, doctor, I keep thinking I'm a pair of curtains!
Pull yourself together.

Doctor, doctor, I've lost my voice!
Now then, what seems to be the trouble?

Doctor, doctor, I think I'm a dog!
Get up on the couch, then, and I'll have a look at you.
I can't, I'm not allowed on the furniture.

Doctor, doctor, people are always ingoring me!
Next!

Doctor, doctor, I keep thinking I'm a tennis racket!
Well, you are rather highly strung.

Doctor, Doctor, I keep thinking I'm a pack of cards!
Sit down, I'll deal with you later.

Quick Groan
How can you tell the time without a watch?
Eat an apple and count the pips!

Don't Ask Me!

What comes out of the sea yelling, "Knickers!"?
Crude oil.

What comes out of the sea yelling, "Panties!"?
Refined oil.

What's red and comes out of the ground at 100 m.p.h.?
An E-type carrot.

What road do policemen live in?
Letsby Avenue!

What goes clip?
A one-legged horse.

What d'you get if you cross John Travolta with the Fonz?
He-ey fever.

What's thick and yellow and very dangerous?
Shark-infested custard.

What's yellow and swings from cake to cake?
Tarzipan.

Quick Groan
What do pixies eat?
Elf foods!

Quick Groan
How d'you get a peanut out of your ear?
Pour in some chocolate and it comes out a treat!

Animal Crackers

Q: What's the best way to catch squirrels?
A: Climb up a tree and act like a nut.

Q: What do you get when you pour boiling water down a rabbit hole?
A: A hot-cross bunny.

Q: What do you give a budgie for breakfast?
A: Tweetabix.

Q: Where do frogs leave their hats?
A: In the croakroom.

Q: What do two elephants play in a Mini?
A: Squash.

Quick Groan
What's green, covered in custard and miserable?
Apple grumble!

A boy took his dog with him to the film of Alice in Wonderland. The dog sat in the seat next to the boy. The usherette came along and noticed the dog sitting. She was just about to throw it out when she saw that it seemed to be watching the film very carefully. So she let it stay. When the film was finished the usherette went over and spoke to the boy.

"I was surprised to see how much your dog enjoyed the show," she said.

"It surprised me, too," the boy answered, "he didn't like the book at all."

THE KIDS ARE ALL RIGHT

That's what Mary-Anne says. And she should know — she's a nursery nurse!

AT eighteen, Mary-Anne Whybrow is a stand-in mum to a dozen energy-packed toddlers — and she loves every hectic minute of it! Mary-Anne's a nursery nurse — she works in a modern nursery on a big estate just outside Birmingham.

There are sixty children on the register, but only about thirty to forty are there on any one day. Ages range from tiny babies to five-year-olds leaving to start infant school.

The one-storey building is divided into a large hall with lots of rooms opening off it — some big like the toddlers' room and the baby wing, others small "activity" rooms with a nursery nurse as assistant in charge.

As you'd expect, each of these rooms is given over to a special activity. There's a television room, a book and puzzles room and a home room, complete with dressing-up clothes. There's even a tot-sized play kitchen and shop!

It's Mary-Anne's job to keep her children healthy, happy and busy — and teach them some skills that'll be useful when they go to school. So finger-painting and sand play, games and stories, Playdough and building bricks are a big part of Mary-Anne's working life. So are birthday parties and cut knees, hugs and sulks, giggles and tears.

With the help of a nursery assistant, Carol, Mary-Anne looks after the kids throughout the day. She decides what play things to get out and supervises play. Mind you, she considers "supervise" far too posh a word!

"There's a lot of nose-wiping and tear-drying and dealing with tantrums and stopping fights as well," she laughs. "You have to get right down to the children's level to see things their way — and Carol and I spend half the day clearing up.

"But I'm in charge and I can use my imagination and do what I want — within reason. I like that.

"For instance, a few weeks ago, I decided to have a nature table, so I cut out pictures at home to bring in and then took a couple of the children out

with me each afternoon to collect leaves and flowers. They loved it all!

"Because some of the children come from deprived homes they don't have the chance to do the everyday things other kids take for granted. So some days when there aren't many kids in, Carol or I will take a couple of them down to the shops or for a walk or for a ride on the bus.

ZOO TIME

"That's apart from the big nursery outings when we all pile into the mini-bus driven by George and go to the zoo or to feed the ducks in the park. You should see the amazement on some of their faces when they see a duck.

"As well as being a treat, I suppose it is all part of teaching the children about life. We don't behave like teachers though. We pick the children up and cuddle them.

"We're like substitute mums and we try to make the nursery

as home-like as possible. Some children are here nearly 12 hours a day, so it *is* almost home for them.

"Sometimes we meet parents too and they tell us about problems with the children. So as well as knowing how to communicate with three-year-olds you have to be able to talk to parents."

Except for Christmas, Easter, bank holidays and weekends, the nursery is open five days a week all year round. Mary-Anne's day starts at 7, 8 or 10 a.m. — depending which shift she's on. There's only a half-hour break during the day.

Here's a run-down of a fairly typical day in the nursery.

7 a.m. Welcome the first arrivals and get their breakfast, because the cook isn't there this early. These early-birds are usually children with only one parent who has to go to work early.

Whoever's not -looking after the toast puts out the playthings, so the other children will have something to

do when they arrive — brought in by mothers or by George in the mini-bus.

The sad side of a nursery like this is that several of the children come from homes where they don't get a great deal of love and attention. A few are "high risk" children, known to be in danger of being ill-treated at home.

UPSETTING

One of Mary-Anne's distressing jobs is to check these children all over for signs of injury and report it to the officer-in-charge or one of her two deputies. She remembers, soon after taking the job, finding a small boy she'd just bathed covered in strange round marks all over his bottom. She rushed to the office, where it was gently pointed out that they were imprints from the rubber bath mat he'd been sitting on!

"It doesn't upset me so much now, but I still sometimes go home worrying about a child," she admitted. "It's hard not to."

11 a.m. Time for all the children to be taken to the toilet and washed ready for lunch in half an hour. If it seems early, you have to remember some of them have been there since seven.

Mary-Anne and Carol have their lunch at a table in the hall with a group of mixed-age children who are their special responsibility at meal times. One two-year-old used a knife and fork as if she'd been born using them; an older boy needed a lot of help; one little girl chattered all the time and wanted a third helping; a new boy refused to eat a mouthful or speak to anyone.

After lunch, the younger children have a nap — the toddlers have folding cots put up in their room. The older ones can play outside, have stories read to them or watch TV. The nurses and assistants get half an hour each to put their feet up in the staff room.

1.45 p.m. The children are woken up and play activities for the afternoon begin. By 3.30 many will have been fetched or taken home. Others will stay till collected any time before 6.30.

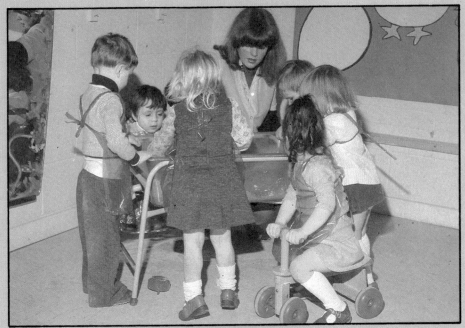

A nursery nurse generally looks after mainly healthy children — aged from six months to seven years old. She plays with them, washes and feeds them, and teaches them to do things for themselves. Nursery nurses work in infant and nursery schools, and in residential and day nurseries run by local authorities.

Some live in — their off-duty periods are arranged so that every member of staff has several evenings off a week, and usually one complete weekend off every month. Nursery nurses can also work as private nannies at home and abroad.

Some children's wards and maternity hospitals employ nursery nurses — to look after the babies and help teach infant care to mothers. Hospitals and homes for handicapped children employ nursery nurses too.

TRAINING

There are two methods of training for school leavers:

1. Two-year courses run by local authorities leading to the certificate awarded by the National Nursery Examination Board. Students spend two-fifths of their training in practical work in nurseries and nursery schools — supervised by qualified staff. The rest of their training is spent at a college of further education where students study all aspects of child care and child development.

2. 18 to 24-month courses at private nursery training colleges affiliated to the Association of Nursery Training Colleges. Students should preferably have some G.C.E. passes and must be at least eighteen years old.

College students learn exactly the same as N.N.E.B. students. In fact, private colleges prepare their students for the N.N.E.B. examinations as well as for their own college diplomas. Nurseries are attached to all private colleges so that students have children to work with.

Private college-training costs between £500 and £1500 for the course, and local education authority grants are sometimes given. One of the advantages of this course is that it sometimes helps you to get a private nursing job.

Further information: National Nursery Examination Board, Argyle House, 29-31 Euston Road, London NW1 2SD, if you live in Northern Ireland, England or Wales.
Contact the Scottish Nursery Nurses Examination Board, 38 Queen Street, Glasgow C1, if you live in Scotland. Local authority education or health and social services departments can help too.
Don't forget to enclose a stamped addressed envelope if you write for information.

Mary-Anne did her two-year training course at Solihull College of Technology. She went there straight from school at sixteen with good "O"-levels and after an interview with two of the course tutors. I asked one of these tutors what she looks for when choosing future nursery nurses.

"The girls must have a realistic view of children, and not see them all as little angels," she said. "I'd expect a girl of sixteen who says she wants to work with children to have got herself some experience, perhaps by baby-sitting or doing voluntary work with children."

Mary-Anne thinks you need to be "lively, energetic, confident, bubbly and able to go down to a child's level." She had experience of baby-sitting with young cousins (she only has one brother and he's older) and decided after a careers talk at school that nursery nursing was the job for her.

"I thought I knew a bit about children, but although I knew *how* they behaved I didn't have a clue *why*. I found that out at college when we did child psychology and development. We got plenty of chance to put it into practice too, because every second week was spent working in a nursery or infant school."

Despite her qualifications, getting a job wasn't easy and many of her forty-five class-mates still haven't found one.

Mary-Anne explained. "You could get a super position as a nanny almost anywhere in the world and I know girls who have done that. But there's a shortage of jobs around here and most people don't want to leave home — not yet anyway."

Her first ambition was to work with babies in a maternity hospital, but there were no openings. She came to the nursery to work in the baby unit and enjoyed it "even though there is a lot of feeding

and nappy changing." Then she was put in charge of the toddlers' room and finds that just as much fun — and even more rewarding.

"You're not supposed to have favourites and I wouldn't let it show, but I tend to give most love and attention to those children I know don't get much at home. There is a little girl who comes in dirty and

with sores on her legs because she's neglected. I bath her, put on new clothes and treat her legs with ointment (they're almost better now) and it's lovely to see her change before your eyes.

"Then we had a boy who never spoke, because he wasn't talked to at home — maybe his mother just didn't think of it or something. We chatted to him non-stop and now he'll hold long conversations with everyone.

"I think the best thing about this job is, when you go home at night, you know you've done something worthwhile."

Continued on page 88

85

Fit For Anything!

We've given these top stars a sporting chance to tell us how they keep fighting fit!

Ian Page, Secret Affair:

"If I could afford it I'd love to have a sauna cabin built at my home so's I could pop into it whenever I fancied.

"I've heard that it makes you feel much fitter and livelier after you've steamed yourself clean.

"And, as far as I'm concerned, the better you can make yourself physically, the better you'll feel mentally."

Chrissie Hynde:

"I'm not a fitness freak at all and so I don't take much exercise.

"I'm lucky really 'cos no matter what I eat, I keep to the same weight.

"My favourite way of toning up is lazing around in a big, deep bath for hours and hours.

"I may not be very energetic — but it feels really nice all the same!"

Patrick Duffy, Dallas:

"I've always found that yoga and meditation help me feel great.

"Every morning I spend about twenty minutes just sitting quietly and thinking about my special Bhuddist chant.

"It helps me to clear my mind of all my worries and problems, and when I'm finished my mind's alert and ready to cope with just about anything!"

Simon Smith, Merton Parkas:

"Even though I'm invited to lots of parties I try to avoid them as much as possible when I'm trying to concentrate on my music.

"I think it's important to get a full night's sleep as regularly as possible.

"You might think that a lot of the people in this business are living it up through the small hours —— but most of them are tucked up soundly in bed before the majority of parties have even started!"

Mick Jagger:

"I always set out on a tour like I'm setting out for the Olympics! After all, athletes have to tune their bodies up to peak performance and so should pop stars.

"I book myself into a gymnasium for a few weeks before the tour and I do lots of strenuous work-outs with weights and exercises."

Suzi Quatro:

"Wherever I go I either take my own fold-up, portable bike or else I hire one in every city that we stop in.

"I love cycling. Not only does it tone up all my muscles but it's also a marvellous feeling to be out in the early morning just riding along quiet, empty streets. It's much better than sitting in a stuffy car!"

Richard O'Sullivan:

"I used to go jogging in the mornings before going to work but it made me feel much worse than usual, so I gave it up and decided to eat a bit less instead!

"You see, all that jogging in the fresh air was making me feel really hungry so I was eating twice as much as I did before!"

Amii Stewart:

"I don't diet very much 'cos I do so much exercise that I seem to burn up all the extra calories I've taken on.

"My way to fitness is dancing. Anyone can do that. Even at home, I stick on the record player and do some energetic dancing exercises. Even just ordinary dancing is enjoyable, and it helps to keep your weight down and also tones up your body."

Continued from page 85

Luckily, something went wrong with Jeff's car the very next day and Mike came round at night to help him . . .

COFFEE'S UP!

NOW FOR THE TEST—THERE'S A DOSE OF POTION IN MIKE'S.

THANKS, VAL—BISCUITS, TOO! YOU MUST'VE KNOWN I WAS STARVING.

OH, YOU'RE SO GORGEOUS . . .

AND I'M DYING OF THIRST . . .

HEY—THAT ONE'S MIKE'S!

IT DOESN'T MATTER, VAL. WE BOTH TAKE THE SAME AMOUNT OF SUGAR.

Before I could stop him Jeff had drained the mug. I wondered what on earth the effect would be . . .

WHEN YOU COME TO THINK OF IT, MIKE—THE OLD GIRL'S WORTH ALL THE TIME WE SPEND ON HER. SHE'S BEAUTIFUL . . . THEY JUST DON'T MAKE 'EM LIKE HER ANY MORE.

PHEW, THAT'S A RELIEF! IT'S JUST MADE HIM MORE INFATUATED WITH HIS TATTY OLD CAR.

ER . . . YOU MUST BE THIRSTY, TOO. LIKE ANOTHER ONE, MIKE?

YES, OK. YOU MAKE SUCH A LOVELY CUP OF COFFEE.

THIS TIME I'LL PUT IN TWICE THE AMOUNT OF POTION TO MAKE DOUBLY SURE.

But . . .

HE . . . HE DRANK IT WITHOUT LOOKING AT ME. DON'T SAY HE'S GOING TO FALL IN LOVE WITH THE CAR, TOO? OH, I'M BEING STUPID— I SHOULD NEVER HAVE BELIEVED IN THAT RUBBISH OF OSSIE'S!

I GUESS I'LL JUST HAVE TO ACCEPT THAT MIKE ISN'T AS INTERESTED IN ME AS I AM IN HIM. AND THERE'S NOTHING I CAN DO ABOUT IT.

Then, the next night, as I was doing my homework . . .

HEY, GUESS WHAT, VAL? THIS AFTERNOON MIKE COLLAPSED AT THE OFFICE AND WAS RUSHED OFF TO HOSPITAL. APPARENTLY HE'S GOT FOOD POISINING.

OH, NO!

QUICK, QUICK! WHICH HOSPITAL'S HE IN?

ST MARTHA'S, WARD THREE. BUT LISTEN . . .

NO—I'VE GOT TO GET THERE RIGHT AWAY!

St Martha's Hospital

I SHOULDN'T HAVE GIVEN HIM DOUBLE THE AMOUNT. WH- WHAT IF SOMETHING DREADFUL HAPPENS TO HIM? OH . . .

Short story by Sue Papworth

ENISTA CELANDINE BROWN, waiting in the rain for someone who probably won't come at all, rain water falling down from the brim of her hat and making a veil of tears across her big shy eyes.

Waiting in the rain, trying to pretend she doesn't know he won't come; telling herself he's delayed, the car broke down, he tried to ring her — but knowing all along he just couldn't be bothered. Feeling, but trying not to feel, foolish, lonely and sad. Too unimportant for someone to make the effort to meet her on a cold, wet evening.

Genista Celandine Brown, not knowing that in the soft, damp, watercolour light, framed in hat and scarf and curling hair, she looked like a flower in the morning rain; that her mother had chosen well when she gave her impossible, silly, embarrassing flower names. Only feeling sad and let down again.

Genni Brown, not yet knowing that she was the most important person in the world, looked at her watch and sighed. She knew she shouldn't have waited. She'd been told often enough never to wait.

But suppose he really had been delayed? She knew he hadn't, but she couldn't leave when he *might* rush up and say, "Genni, I'm sorry . . ."

Just when she thought she'd leave him for ever, he always turned to her and said how he needed her — or just how she'd misunderstood, and he'd never really *promised* . . . And she always came back, to be hurt, again.

Why am I so silly, she thought? You try to live as if all the world were kind and polite and thoughtful — and they're not. You know it really, but won't admit it.

But I thought he was different, she argued back.

You were wrong again. He thinks he can pick you up and drop you as he pleases.

Perhaps he's right, she thought sadly. She looked down at her wet feet, saw the rain forming pools in the cracked paving stones, heard it tapping on the rooftops and road. But slowly she realised that the tapping behind her wasn't only the rain. She turned and the boy, looking at her from a few feet away through rain-streaked glass, smiled so gently she forgot to be startled. A wall of red-framed glass pushed out towards her, and he beckoned. "You're getting soaked. Come in. Wait in here."

She found herself inside, closed off from the rain, squeezed against a wall of the phone box. She pulled off her hat and shook out her hair. They smiled.

Continued on page 92

TEARS AS SOFT AS SUMMER RAIN...

Continued
from page 91

TEARS AS SOFT AS SUMMER RAIN...

"You're waiting for someone?"

She nodded, but he saw she didn't look out.

"He shouldn't keep you waiting, not in this rain. Not ever. I wouldn't," he said softly.

She looked up at him in surprise and saw tiny water drops in curling auburn hair, exactly the colour of her own; laughing green eyes in a serious face.

"What's your name?" she said, trying not to smile, trying not to think of Peter — perhaps struggling with his car, perhaps at home with a record on the stereo.

"Leo."

She smiled now.

"And yours?" he asked.

"Genista Celandine Brown."

Why had she told him? Usually she said Genni. People laughed such a lot.

He laughed — but it was pure delight.

"Genista Celandine Brown! Perfect! Lovely wild flowers where you don't expect to find them. On a moor — or in a phone box, in the rain. Who are you waiting for, and must you?"

She shrugged. "There'll be a reason. There always is. He . . . often can't come. He has an important job. He's often very busy . . ." her voice trailed off.

"So he leaves you to wait in the rain?"

She looked out of the window. "I suppose it's my fault for waiting. I always wait."

"Why?"

"I . . . we're supposed to be engaged. Everyone says how lucky I am. He has got a car and a flat and a good job and . . ."

". . . he leaves you to wait in the rain."

He saw the tears come to her eyes.

"I'm sorry. Please don't."

His arm was round her, and she felt a soft hankie pressed into her hand with gentle clumsiness.

"Don't cry. Look, why don't you ring him? I could get you a taxi if you like . . ."

She heard his concern, and it made it impossible to hold back the tears. He held her gently while she cried. He didn't seem to mind her soaked coat and wet hair.

At length she stopped, choking back the last sobs.

"I . . . I'm sorry . . . I shouldn't . . . I didn't mean to . . . I'm so unhappy and confused."

"Flowers need warmth and care," he said. He touched her hair tenderly.

"Genista. Why didn't I meet you before?"

She smiled gently.

"It's never rained so hard before," she said.

A harsh, strident sound broke in on them. She turned, and looked out. Peter's car was across the road, the horn sounding, forty minutes late.

As she stood, still inside the phone box, Genista could see Peter looking over towards her. He hadn't got out of the car, but he'd pushed the passenger door open. He pressed the horn again, impatiently. He didn't like to be kept waiting.

Leo turned to her, and held out his umbrella.

"Genista Celandine Brown, can I offer you a lift anywhere?"

"Anywhere?" she asked, smiling.

He smiled back.

She stepped out beside him, and heard the rain patter cheerfully down above them. As the phone box door closed, Leo put his arm round her to hold her close in the shelter of the big, black umbrella.

"I think you were waiting for something," he said, as they walked off under the silver clouds.

"Yes," she said. "You."

FAMOUS LAST WORDS

. . . positively the last word on
how to get the last word!

LAST words just aren't enough, they've got to be **FAMOUS LAST WORDS!** ''Oops, sorry'' just doesn't have the impact you need when you zap out of this life, out of your latest, wildest love affair, out of your favourite jeans, draughtily in the High Street.

Of course, being the one who always gets the last word in any exchange is something that has to be worked at.

Take, for example, when your romance goes stale on you, when the mad beautiful fling deteriorates into a constant bicker and you realise that it's going to end soon. You mustn't get sentimental about how it used to be and let HIM get the last vicious remark in. That will only make things worse for you – not only will you realise that you've been emotionally had, but you'll get a sharp reminder that when a boy gets bitchy, he gets really bitchy – even bitchier than you!

So remember, don't weaken as your romance dwindles to its last parting moments, and don't let him have the final evil remark. It will only leave you wincing for weeks.

Of course, it isn't just boys you're up against. It's things, too. You've got the whole universe against you, remember that. It's good to know these things.

Sometimes, it's as if there's some force out there just waiting with curled lip for you to get too stroppy.

You've only got to boast about something once and it'll strike. You've had a pair of tights last three weeks. Now you know in your heart that you ought to keep quiet about it, but it isn't the same if you don't boast to someone about this minor triumph in your life. So you do.

As soon as the words are out, as soon as they have passed your lips, you're doomed! The tights won't last another three minutes, the next step you take and – rip, they'll be goners.

WHEN it comes to actual last words though, there's one person who's best at delivering the kind of insult that leaves you gasping – your best friend! This is because you

IT'S ONLY A BAD HEAD COLD . . .

think that you have a best friend. But in fact when it comes to looks and loves you're on your own, and the relationship you have with all other females is nearer to war.

So when you're feeling pretty good about your new hairstyle, and not on your guard, it's easy for your pal to come across with, ''I like your hair. It really hides your funny neck.'' Whammo. The words hang stinging in the air, and will stay with you for years.

You'll ask a succession of fellas, ''What's wrong with my neck?'' They'll gaze at you amazed; they'd never really looked at your neck and it won't make any difference to you now, even if they keep on telling you how lovely your neck is. Secretly, you'll believe forever that there's something odd about it.

The only thing for it is to have a selection of famous last words of your own – all ready to lash back when someone lays a nasty remark on you.

This is absolutely necessary because you know that if you leave it to your ready wits, you won't think of a swift and cutting reply till you're round the corner or sitting on the bus back home.

One fairly good trick is to act deaf. When the fella you love and have loved for the last few months finally tells you that it's over, and furthermore you get on his nerves and he never wants to see you again ever ever ever – your best plan is to look slightly glazed, tilt your head to one side and say, ''Pardon?''

By the time he has repeated his passionate parting speech three times it will have lost its impact. He'll say, ''Aw, forget it,'' and wander off.

Alternatively, if snippy replies and devious ruses fail you, a loud raspberry is always good. Well, it is absolutely unanswerable – and good fun to make, too!

THERE are some folk who just never accept that their famous last words are their famous last words. You know the sort of thing. They see the love of their life with another girl. ''Oh, they're just friends,'' they say. The lovers take hands. ''Oh,'' says the optimist, ''they only want to keep cosy. She's forgotten her gloves.'' And on and on and on. All the way to the weeping on the pillow and the heartache.

It's understandable that anyone would go on hoping, clinging on to what they've got because they don't want to utter that most famous last word of all – goodbye.

Ah well, it's almost time for us to say goodbye. Ta ta, so long and all that stuff. Last words are sad, aren't they? Not nearly so tasty as first words – hello, well hi, how do you do, and wotcher! There's lotsa promise in first words.

Words, words, words . . . we've got lots of them in Blue Jeans. We've got nice words, silly words, cheeky words, slushy words galore, true words and help-you-over-bad-times words of wisdom.

So we'll let our last words here be not so much a goodbye, more a see you – every week in **BLUE JEANS . . .**

PSSST—ARE WE POISONOUS? Y'SEE, I'VE JUST BITTEN MY LIP . . .

July

Holiday time is here! Are *you* going to get the most out of it?

  b. Well, of course. I'm going to Bournemouth with Auntie and Uncle and my grotty cousins like I always do.
  c. Of course. I've been saving like mad for this super holiday in this super new place with these super people . . . .
  a. Of course. I'm going to stop snoozing in this chair *here* and go and snooze in a deckchair *there*.

August

After you've tottered back home, laden with sticks of rock and raffia donkeys and eighteen tons of seashells, what do you do?

  c. Finish off my Christmas shopping, re-plan my winter wardrobe, re-decorate my bedroom and start an exciting new job.
  a. Sit about saying, "Woe! Summer is over, and now there's nothing to look forward to, only horrible, boring, cold, dull winter."
  b. Stick my holiday snaps all around the walls, and make an effort to keep my tan going as long as possible.

September

The leaves are turning to gold upon the trees, but there are still warm, sunny days. How are you passing your time?

  c. Drafting next year's New Year Resolutions, going dancing, being sent to New York by my firm, being interviewed on television, and writing a novel in my spare time.
  a. Wondering where the summer went.
  b. Making the most of the long evenings.

October

As the mornings begin to have a frosty sparkle, your breath turns white upon the air, and Hallowe'en approaches, how are you keeping up with the hurrying year?

  a. With great difficulty.
  b. What? Oh, OK, but right now I'm too busy making toffee apples and gingerbread men.
  c. I'm planning my Easter holiday visit to the people I met on holiday last July.